Getting *into* Yale

How One Student Wrote *THIS* Book and Got Into the School of His Dreams

Josh Berezin

A Seth Godin Production

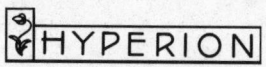

Library of Congress Cataloging-in-Publication Data
Berezin, Josh, 1979–
    Getting into Yale : how one student wrote this book (and got into the school of his dreams) / Josh Berezin. — 1st ed.
       p.   cm.
    Includes index.
    ISBN 0-7868-8302-2 (alk. paper)
    1. Universities and colleges—United States—Admission.
2. Berezin, Josh, 1979–   —Diaries.   3. High school seniors—United States—Diaries.   4. Yale University—Admission.   I. Title.
LB2351.2.B425   1998   97-39252
378.1'61'0973—dc21   CIP

FIRST EDITION

10 9 8 7 6 5 4 3 2 1

Contents

▶

Preface ix

The Background on Me xi

Part One
Falling in Love with Yale 1

Part Two
Apply Yourself 39

Part Three
Waiting 113

Part Four
The Final Moments 149

Epilogue 157

Author's Note (and Reader's Cheat Sheet) 163

Dedication

►

To Mom, Dad, and Rachael

Acknowledgments

▶

First of all, I would like to thank all those who contributed to this project. First and foremost, thanks to Seth Godin, Karen Watts, Sarah Silbert, Emily Gold, and the rest of the crew at SGP whose patience and enthusiasm never waned, and without whom the seed for this project would never have been planted. Thanks also to David Cashion at Hyperion—without him it would never have bloomed.

Second, I would like to thank all of my friends, relatives, and teachers who contributed not only to this book but to my life during this crucial and stressful time. Thanks to Mr. Rankin, Mr. Schutter, Mr. Pollack, Mrs. Blattner, Aaron McMickle, Elena Casal, Emily West (who was a really good sport), Phil Toomajian, Shellie Calland, Coach Kornblut, Coach Sedmak, Tamara Shirdak, Ken Cohen, Alec Berezin, Marcia Berezin, and Rachael Berezin.

Third, I would like to thank the many people who helped me get into college. This includes a list of people longer than the book itself, but I would like to mention a few in particular. In addition to those mentioned above, thanks to every teacher I ever had, especially Mrs. Hosmer, Mr. Gross, Mrs. Merchant, Mr. Foote, and Mrs. MacDonald. Each of them challenged me to think critically and to expand my intellectual horizons. For those gifts I am forever thankful. A very special thanks to Mrs. Blattner for the tremendous help she gave me during the application process and throughout high school. Thanks to every coach I ever had, especially Coach Kornblut (who always encouraged and stood behind me), Coach Horstman (who constantly pushed me and showed me what it meant to be intense), the rest of the football staff (especially Coach Q and Coach Fello), and thanks most of all to Coach Sedmak, who taught me more about myself than he can ever imagine, and who I respect almost more than any other person.

Thanks to all my friends. There's no way I could mention even half the friends who have affected my life. Just let me say thanks to all of you—hopefully you know who you are—and acknowledge a few in particular: Very special thanks to Rob Emerich, Alex Hamerstone, Lyndsey Mirmelstein, and all of my past teammates, especially the class of '97 football team. I appreciate the friendship and support you have all given me over the years.

Thanks to all my family, extended and otherwise. Thanks to my cousins (Sheryl, Raffie, David, Mickey, Jerome, Leslie, Robin, and all your families), my aunts and uncles (Aunty Joe and Uncle Ziggy, Auntie Judy, and especially Uncle Kenny and Aunt Debby), and all the other crazy relatives that make up the Berezin/Cohen family. Oh yeah, and thanks to Mom, Dad, and Rachael. You guys are the best.

My sincerest apologies to the fifty people I did not mention. Please do not feel slighted and be sure to call me and make me feel guilty for not saying how grateful I am to you.

Preface

▶

I've been thinking about college ever since my sister applied three years ago. She was a bright student who never really applied herself and therefore was limited in her choice of schools. After witnessing that, I decided to make sure I had the choices she didn't. By junior year, thinking about college took up even more of my time—hardly a day went by when thoughts about it weren't on my mind. Everyday in at least one of my classes there would be some discussion of where someone was looking, who was getting in where, or how to get in. It was almost fun for a while, but it got very old, very fast. There were days when I would cover my ears and sing a song when someone started talking about it, like two-year-olds do when they don't feel like talking to their parents. Other times I would snap that I was dropping out of high school and working in McDonald's in Toledo for the rest of my life, okay? I realize this isn't the most mature way to deal with people, but sometimes it got to be a little much. I'm not the only one who feels this way, either. I've had conversations with the top people in my class who said they'd felt the same way—and that was junior year! I can't imagine how I am going to get through this one. Forget about the talk; I'll actually have to apply.

When I was younger, I thought my senior year of high school would be one long party. I would be captain of the football and wrestling teams, get a lot of girls, have a car, and I wouldn't have to worry about college anymore. Actually, the plan is mostly working out except for the part about worrying about college and the part about getting the girls. I also thought that senior year would be very easy, academically, I mean, but right now I am scheduled to take six AP courses, two more than in junior year. I'm already ready for it to be over.

Maybe once I get into a college, I'll feel better. At least I'll be able to attend family gatherings and not have to worry about getting asked where I want to go. I'm never really sure what to say. The unfortunate thing is, when people ask you what your first choice is, and you say a school like Yale, they immediately assume that if you're good enough to be talking about going there, you're good enough to get in. I counteract that reaction by immediately following up with: I want to go to Yale *but* I'm not sure if I can get in so I'll probably end up at University of Michigan, which, don't get me wrong, would be a wonderful place to live and learn for four years. At a bar mitzvah last weekend, my eleven-year-old cousin just happened to be by me every time someone asked the dreaded question. By the end of the weekend, he had heard my little speech so many times that I just referred all inquiries to him. The problem with constantly telling people I'm not good enough to get in is that I am almost starting to believe it. The whole idea of applying to college, and having someone you've never met read about you for five minutes and proceed to make a decision that will affect the rest of your life, seems a little ridiculous, not to mention discouraging. I mean, if that guy doesn't like what he sees, then you're screwed. It's confusing to have to sort through all of these emotions, so the one that I have been settling on lately has been apathy. Sometimes the whole thing gets so overwhelming that the easiest thing to do is to pretend that I don't care what happens.

But I do care. I want to go to Yale as much as I've wanted anything before. And I have experience in getting what I want. Like being the smallest offensive lineman on the football team. Granted Yale's a bit different, seeing as it's not really in my control. But I'm a really determined guy, and when I set my sights on something, I'm usually able to achieve it (with the unfortunate exclusions of winning wrestling matches and getting girls). And right now I'm set on *getting into Yale*.

The Background
on Me

▶

At the end of junior year, the guidance office requests that each student put together a little personal history, so the counselors have an idea what to say on their recommendations. This is what I turned in.

I was born on June 8, 1979, which makes me 17 years old now. My parents' names are Alec and Marcia. I have one older sister, Rachael, who will be 21 in October, although she sometimes acts like she's three.

Until sixth grade, I went to a small, private school called Hawken. When we ran out of money, we moved into an apartment in a suburb of Cleveland, and I now attend Shaker Heights High School. I've played football since I was in seventh grade and have wrestled since eighth grade. I also played tennis in the middle school, but when I realized that continuing this would result in my getting a royal ass-beating in the football locker room, I decided to end my illustrious tennis career before high school. I have received many, many trophies and T-shirts from my involvement with football. It would take a long time to list them, but most are to the effect of "Camper of the Week," "Ironman of the Week," or "Quest for Excellence Second Place in Points Earned." My grades in high school have been consistently good since freshman year, and would be higher if I hadn't been so lazy that year. I have taken the SATs, the Modern European History, U.S. History, and Chemistry Advanced Placement exams, and four SAT IIs (formerly known as

Achievement Tests) in Biology, U.S. History, Math, and Writing. I plan to use the knowledge gained in studying for these exams to overthrow the Educational Testing Service, which institutes all of these standardized tests.

I have made decent use of my summer time. After freshman year, I went on Outward Bound for three weeks in the North Carolina mountains. Last year I spent about 30 hours volunteering in a local children's hospital. The rest of my summers were, and are, being spent lifting and running in preparation for football and wrestling seasons.

Part One

▶

Falling
in Love
with Yale

7/1/96—I didn't even want to see Yale . . .

I didn't even want to see Yale. When we were going East looking at colleges, I had already seen Harvard and I figured that Yale would probably be about the same: disappointing. I had heard all these wonderful things about the amazing people who go to Harvard and the amazing people who have been going there for hundreds of years, but it really wasn't all that. In any case, Yale was not top on my list.

We went to the information session that most schools have before the tour. About five minutes into the talk, I realized I had been all wrong. This was where I wanted to go. It wasn't that the guy who was giving us his spiel was so great—in fact, he was probably the worst I've heard. And the student they brought in to assure us that it wasn't *that* hard to get in and that New Haven wasn't *that* bad was no more enthusiastic than anywhere else. I guess it was mostly what the main guy, whose name was Josh Auerbach (I remember his name because his first name is the same as mine and his last is the same as a girl in my high school), said about what they were looking for in a Yale student. Everything he said about Yalies seemed to be an accurate description of myself. He talked about how Yale students loved to argue vehemently about something, but then go out and play Frisbee. He talked about looking for the type of people whose families went to art museums not because parents dragged their kids along but because the kids dragged their parents.

Whatever it was, I was hooked, and so was my dad. As we were waiting for the tour to start, we hoped the campus would be ugly so I would hate it—we didn't want to like it *too* much and be *too* disappointed if I didn't get in. Well, much to our dismay, the campus was unbelievable. You couldn't tell the difference between the cathedral and the Economics Building. They all looked like they were built in France 400 years ago and shipped to New Haven where the ivy rooted them to the ground. I had the same feeling on the tour that I did during the info session—I wanted to go to this school real bad. But there was one last thing my father and I knew would be essential in finding the school for me: really good food. Well, of course I had the best calzone *ever* in a restaurant about five minutes away from campus. In his excitement, my dad made reservations for a party of ten for the fall of 1997, so he could take me and my friends out for dinner.

I was not quite as optimistic—or unrealistic—as my dad. I knew plenty of people who applied last year, were very well qualified, but did not get in. In fact, the only person I know who did was a swimmer and was recruited. I'm nowhere near being big enough or good enough to play football at Yale, and I have no desire to wrestle in college. This, and the fact that every college guide book says that Yale is beyond tough to get into, made me feel very apprehensive. But I also sort of had a good feeling about the whole thing. I felt like I had fallen in love with Yale, and it seemed only natural that Yale would fall in love with me.

➤

Marcia Berezin
Mother

I didn't have the same initial reaction to Yale as Josh and his dad did. I liked it, but it didn't strike me, maybe because we had visited so many colleges before. But the campus was beautiful and there was no dimming Josh's enthusiasm for the place. I had learned from Rachael and some of her friends that kids somehow seem to know when they get to a school where they really feel comfortable. You can't argue with that—and as a parent you shouldn't.

It made me nervous that Yale is so hard to get into. People would say to me, "Don't you think he'll get in?" And I said, "Well, he's just one of many. And, yes, he's qualified, but every other person who's applying really has great qualifications, too." It made me really nervous.

The day after I got home, I went to football practice. All the guys and coaches asked me how it went, and I told them how awesome Yale was. It was nice to be excited about something again. My junior year was the toughest of my life. My routine for most of the school year was waking up, going to school, going to practice (football or wrestling), going to the library to study, going home to study some more, and then going to bed. Going, going, going. I dealt with it pretty well first semester, but once wrestling season started, it got harder to deal with. I was wrestling Junior Varsity behind a state champ and his state-plac-

ing twin brother. Wrestling is tough under normal conditions—
kind of like running a marathon while you have the flu and then
ramming your face into a wall ten times. Add four AP classes to
this grueling physical routine, and you've got yourself one crappy winter. By the time the season ended, I was actually happy to
be able to go home and do my homework every night. That's
pretty sad. Fortunately that only lasted until I finished my APs—
after that, I was done for the year. I figured that I deserved a
break. Translated: I had about as much motivation as a piece of
burned toast. Of course I realized that eventually I was going to
have to study for finals. Unfortunately, I didn't have that realization until about two days before they arrived. Luckily, my year's
worth of hard work paid off, and I ended up with all As (which
pushed my cumulative GPA up to what my sister calls an
"obnoxious" 4.3). Football is the only thing I stayed positive
about while everything else was going to hell. Finally, after
returning from Yale, I was excited about something again, and it
felt good.

But my initial optimism was short-lived. After my workout
(which was unusually hard for an early summer workout), I went
to see my guidance counselor, Mrs. Blattner. I've known her for
a while; she dated my uncle before I was born, so I feel like I can
trust her to give me sound advice. The meeting went well . . . for
a good minute and a half. At first, she was excited that I liked
Yale so much and seemed to share in my enthusiasm. Then she
asked me what I was doing for the summer. I told her I was
working out for the football team every day and that I would be
wrestling at least three days a week. Therefore I didn't really have
time for a steady job. As I spoke I noticed her face begin to sag a
little, but at that time I was somewhat unfazable and continued,
saying I was going to go across the hall to the guidance counselor
who coordinated community service for the high school. Mrs.

Blattner was now in a full-fledged frown—she even started shaking her head. No, clearly this would not do. I needed a hook, something unique and special, not just everyday volunteerism. I needed to get involved with Junior Council on World Affairs or the debate club. Now my face joined hers in a frown. I explained to her that football starts right after school and I'm lucky if it's over by seven, and that was the end of that, in my mind. But not in hers, apparently. She started to tell me how I was putting football over college admission. She said it would be different if I was going to play there or even wrestle in college. She pushed the issue some more and, get this, hinted that maybe I should *quit playing.*

I was speechless. I couldn't believe that someone who knows me would even *think* about suggesting that. Football was the one thing I'd always done with complete passion and total dedication. I tried to explain to her that if I was going to quit the team, I might as well just not go to school anymore. Besides, it seems to me that it would look terrible on a college application if I stopped doing something that I loved in favor of joining some pointless club I don't even care about. Finally she said she understood and, with that in mind, the next best thing would be to find something to do over the summer. Did my parents know any doctors I could work with? My dad had sued a few good doctors and I thought I could probably find one who could help me out. I had tried that last year, though, and wasn't incredibly successful. I ended up volunteering at a local hospital, playing games with kids and helping them adjust to hospital life. She said that was wonderful but not quite wonderful enough. Basically, she said I would have to find something else or my chance for admission would be almost none.

By the time I left, I was a little pissed off at her and really pissed off at myself. I was mad at myself because I should have gotten my summer together during those weeks after my AP exams instead of sitting on my couch eating Ben and Jerry's and watching *The Simpsons*. But I was frustrated with Mrs. Blattner because she knew that even before I fell in love with Yale, I at least wanted to go to Stanford. How was she thinking I would have gotten in *there*? Maybe she could have said something a little earlier than mid-June or mentioned the possibility to my mom when she called for ideas of what I should do this summer. (Instead Mrs. Blattner suggested I talk to the woman in charge of coordinating community service, which would have gotten me another job volunteering, probably in the same hospital, doing the same thing.) In any case, the thing that pissed me off the most was that she was probably right. I had good grades and scores, but I didn't really have anything spectacular to put me head and shoulders above all of the other thousands of people applying to Yale. I went home dejected and depressed . . . but not defeated.

►

Mrs. Blattner
Guidance Counselor

I remember the conversation where Josh told me wanted to go to Yale perfectly. He came into my office and I told him, Josh, you have to do things that are going to make you stand out—to take you from the "no" pile to the "maybe." He was furious with me because he wanted to do his football stuff, but I knew that athletics were not going to get him into Yale—he was going to have to do something different. He didn't want to hear about it. I advised him to use his time doing summer research or something in a field that he might want to pursue. I didn't tell him to quit the football team, but I did tell him that he shouldn't be spending so much time on summer practice.

I really try to advise kids to make whatever they do to get into college something that's going to benefit them anyway.

The two things that I love more than anything else are over-achieving and proving somebody wrong. So I made some phone calls and thought I had found some people who could help me. But one after another they called back and told me how late it was to be doing this and that I had little chance of getting a position that other people had applied for in February. The one person who responded enthusiastically told me to look for a position in the hospital where I worked last year.

Since this discouraging quest of a week ago, I've decided that I'm going to do what I had originally planned to do: play football, wrestle, and volunteer for Habitat for Humanity. I've also decided to read a lot. I know I'm going to be a doctor, so I figure that I'll be doing research for many a summer to come, but I might not have too many more summers when I can come home and read a book. I also plan to do something I don't generally get to do during the year—see movies, go to parties, hang with my friends, and come home (maybe even go out) after midnight. Think of it: a high school kid with a social life.

While I was coming up with this genius plan, though, my dad was devising some of his own. He suggested I call a friend of the family who is in publishing in New York. This guy apparently has a reputation for being a little bit crazy, and my dad thought he might be able think of something that would get Yale's attention. Like so many of my father's ideas, this thought seemed completely inane and a waste of time. (Another example of this inanity is the time he made me take about an hour out of my study time the weekend before exams to look for Brown's roster, based on his conviction that I would be big enough to play football at Brown or Columbia. Of course, when we finally found the stupid roster, the kids who played my position were, at the absolute least, six or seven inches taller and 50 pounds heavier than I.) But despite the seeming futility of his suggestions, my dad can be quite convincing. (Actually maybe he just bothers you about something until he gets his way.) I finally caved in and e-mailed his friend asking for ideas, partly out of curiosity, but mostly to show Dad he was wrong.

From: JBezin@aol.com
To: Friend@aol.com
Re: My Dad's Annoying Idea

Hello, this is Josh Berezin. I hope that you remember who I am (our parents are friends, you used to torture me when I was little). There's a rather lengthy and boring story about why I'm e-mailing you, but I'll try to be brief. I'm 17 and just completed my junior year of high school. Recently my mom and dad and I went East looking at colleges, and I saw Yale and was impressed to say the least. Well, actually, I decided right then I wanted to go there. When I returned home to tell my guidance counselor that Yale was my first choice, she told me it would be hard if not impossible for me to get into Yale without some project this summer or something that would look stellar on my application. I was planning to do some volunteer work along with football and wrestling, but she's pretty sure that won't be enough to get me in. So when I went home and asked my parents if they had any ideas, my father suggested that I contact to you.

After talking to your mother, the consensus was that you were crazy enough to think of something for me to do. I didn't really think that you would have something, but after days and days of hocking from my dad (my father is a great guy but can be extremely annoying when he thinks, usually mistakenly, that he has a good idea), I decided to give in and contact you. If you can think of anything that would look stellar on a college application, please e-mail me right away. Thank you very much.

Well, this guy responded with a list of 13 things I could do:

From: Friend@aol.com
To: JBezin@aol.com
Re: Re: My Dad's Annoying Idea

Well, you could:

1. Come to New York and work with me as a summer intern.
2. Start your own business from scratch. Write a business plan and do ads and make a little money and write the whole thing up in an annual report that you send to Yale with your application.
3. Start a volunteer group that goes through poor neighborhoods in Cleveland—maybe ten guys from your football team—and in one day cleans up some old person's house and paints it or fixes it up. Do one house a week for the whole summer.
4. Teach yourself how to build web pages and start building them for free for volunteer and nonprofit organizations in your town.
5. Pick an industry and research it and write a 30-page pamphlet for college seniors looking for jobs in that industry.
6. Write a short story and get it published.

7. Start a weekly e-newsletter about what's hot and what's not on AOL.

8. Wire your dad's law firm to the Internet and teach everyone how it will make their lives better.

9. Learn Russian.

10. Take a topic you like, like painting, interview a dozen artists around the world, and turn it into an audio collage.

11. Devote the entire summer to breaking a record in *The Guinness Book of World Records.* Then you could write a wonderful essay about it.

12. Create a magazine about rock and roll, find advertisers, then sell it in front of the Rock and Roll Hall of Fame.

13. Borrow $100 from your dad, spend your savings on a one-way ticket to India, fly there, and spend two months living on your wits, then figure out some way to get home.

14. Call the admissions office at Harvard (no need to bother those nice folks at Yale) and come right out and ask them what you should do this summer. Sometimes the direct approach works.

From: JBezin@aol.com
To: Friend@aol.com
Re: Re: Re: My Dad's Annoying Idea

Thanks for the ideas. India is a little far for me and I don't know if I can find a weight room there. My coach likes us to lift weights every Monday, Wednesday, and Friday and run on Tuesdays and Thursdays. Besides, I hear the food isn't that great.

The one about *The Guinness Book of World Records* would

have won hands down—in seventh grade. Most of the suggestions seemed a little far-fetched for me (to tell the truth, my mom negged India right away), but I was beginning to get the picture: Getting into Yale is a challenge—no, a dare. It's a chance for me to put myself over the top and prove *everybody* wrong. I was busy mulling over that revelation today, when I got a call from an editor who works with my dad's friend. She saw our e-mail exchange and thinks it would be great if I kept a journal of my college application process—maybe I'll get in and maybe I won't, but I'll have a really great essay topic for sure, and she thinks there might even be a book in it. I got off the phone totally thrown. Almost in a trance, I went and told my parents. My mom thinks the whole thing is absolutely hilarious. Dad seems to find a lot of humor in it also, though I'm not sure if he's happy that I may be a published author or just basking in the glory of having one of his ideas actually pan out. So that's what has been going on for the past couple of weeks—my dad's been annoying me, and I may have found a hook for Yale.

7/3/96—They say the scores don't matter . . .

Every time somebody is supposed to pick me up, I get worried. I don't even think anyone actually has ever stood me up, but for some reason, that's just one of those things I'm completely paranoid about. Like last night I was supposed to go see *Independence Day* with Phil, someone whom I was good friends with all through middle school. (I used to sleep over at his house every weekend. We had a tradition of watching rented movies—*Basic Instinct* was a highlight of our early-adolescent lives—and making gross pancakes the next morning. Our worst were probably the banana–peanut butter batch. We kind of grew apart during high school, though, mostly because we got involved in different things. But I digress.) So last night, Phil called around 5:30 and told me that he was going to pick me up in a couple of hours. When 7:30 rolled around, though, he wasn't there. It's not that I don't trust him, but immediately I figured that he had stood me up.

►
Phil
Middle School Friend

Josh and I met in middle school. . . . He was small and seemed really frazzled and a little frustrated. Frazzled is still a good word for Josh. I don't think he's frustrated so much anymore. I think he handles things a lot better, though his room's still a mess.

Of course he showed up at around 7:45. All that frustration for nothing. We picked up our friend Mike and then went to the movies. On the way, they started talking about how we were supposed to meet some girls at the theater, which was news to me. I asked who, and wasn't really surprised to find out that Emily and her friends were going to be there.

Emily. Talk about frustration. This is probably one of the most confusing girls who has ever walked the Earth. I started liking her last spring and have been trying to get something going with her for a while. She was in my bio class sophomore year but I didn't meet her or even know her name until we ended up driving home from some girl's birthday party together. Eventually I changed seats in class so I sat behind her and we started talking. Last fall I finally decided that I was going to lay it all on the line and tell her how I felt. I got the opportunity one night when I was out with her and a couple of her friends, when some kid that neither of us knew asked how long we had been seeing each other. Everyone in school had already asked me this question. Emily and I had gone to Homecoming together and been exchanging goofy smiles and giggling in the halls, so naturally everyone, including me (but apparently not including her), thought we were going out.

Well, after this kid asked her that, Emily got a little embarrassed and left the room. I figured that this was a good sign. So that night I offered to give her a ride home. When we got to her driveway I asked her what she thought about what he had asked. I don't remember what she said exactly, but we ended up talking for over an hour. I didn't even think about touching her—okay, maybe I thought about it, but I definitely wouldn't have acted on those thoughts. Anyway, the general impression I got from the conversation was that she didn't particularly want to get involved in a relationship—with anyone—but that she shared my feelings.

When I got home that night, I was a very happy camper. Soon after our conversation, though, things changed. She stopped waiting for me after classes, wasn't as nice to me as she had been, started flirting with other guys, stuff like that. This shift unfortunately coincided with the beginning of wrestling season, another huge blow to my ego. Wrestling has a tendency to be kind of emotionally exhausting for me (I don't know, maybe it's the one-loss-after-another thing), so I didn't have the time, energy, or self-confidence to deal with Emily's apparent disinterest.

By the time wrestling season was over, I heard that she was seeing some sophomore, whom I have never talked to or even seen outside of school—but who really annoys me nonetheless. I had my AP exams to deal with, which, like wrestling season, gave me another good excuse not to think about her. She started being really nice to me again, though, and touching me whenever we would see each other. (Nothing serious, just a pat on the back every once in a while.) I was extremely reluctant to engage her. Whenever she gave me a hug or touched me on the arm, I would shy away. I figured, for one thing, that it didn't work when I had been really nice and touchy-feely with her, so I might as well be a little mean. Also, I was trying my best to get over her. A whole year is a long time to have a crush on someone with nothing coming from it. Besides, she had confused the hell out of me, so I thought I might as well return the favor. Again, this is an extremely mature and adult way to deal with this type of situation. To make a long story short, I still can't get over this girl.

Anyway, last night we were supposed to meet her and a few of her friends to see a movie, but we got there too late, missed them, and had to catch the next show. It's probably better that way.

►

Emily
Junior-Year Crush

I met Josh in my biology class in tenth grade. We both loved to talk a lot. He was smart, funny, and a really good student; he was always upset if he got less than an A. I was always pissed because I got Cs. I was shyer then, so it took at least half a year for us to become friends.

Josh and I went to Homecoming and on three dates together. Though I definitely thought about liking him, I considered him more a friend than a boyfriend. His friendship was more important to me, I guess.

Yesterday afternoon I dropped in to see my guidance counselor to tell her what was going on with my little journal scheme for Yale. She was jazzed about it. I realized it was probably wrong of me to be mad at her for not telling me sooner that I needed to do something out of the ordinary this summer. After all, she has about 100 students whom she's responsible for and was just trying to warn me to not be disappointed if and when I got rejected. Or maybe I'm just feeling really positively toward her because she told me that this project would definitely help my chances for admissions.

►

Mrs. Blattner
Guidance Counselor

When Josh first told me about the book, I said "good for you." Off the record, I was thinking, God, this is exactly what I meant. Stand out. Do something that makes you different. I thought if anybody can pull this off, Josh can.

I also told her about my SAT II scores (which I received last night). I got a 720 in Math, a 760 in History, and a 660 in Writing. I already have a 730 in Biology. That 660 on the writing exam is causing me quite a bit of anxiety. My college guide books say that Yale requires any three SAT IIs, so obviously I won't even show them that one. The thing is, one of my other choices, Columbia, requires the writing exam. The ETS has a way that you can release some scores while not releasing others, so my question was whether I should retake it in the fall, and if it was possible to release one set of scores to one school and a different set to another. Mrs. Blattner said to retake the writing test and to release the score only after I had submitted my application. It was a fairly simple answer, and I'm sure that usually I would not have had any problem coming up with it myself. But when I'm thinking about college, suddenly any small problem signals a panic attack.

It kind of annoys me that I have gotten caught up in the

whole numbers game. SATs, SAT IIs, PSATs, APs . . . the only number that I really should be concerned with is my grade point average. That number actually represents all of the hard work I have put into high school since my sophomore year began. The other ones represent what bubbles I filled in on tests that just don't seem to measure much of anything besides how well I can fill in those bubbles. Colleges will tell you that the scores don't matter as much as everyone says, but that's probably bullshit. Because after saying that test scores aren't the deciding factor, college representatives (almost without exception) will go on to admit that they—especially the SAT score—are the second most important aspect of the application. So of course people like me get confused. Colleges say one thing and mean another. Sometimes I think they're doing it on purpose and that the people who can decipher the true message get in. (Actually, that is probably pretty close to the truth.) Like I said, it annoys me that I've gotten so caught up in the numbers, but what else can I do? I didn't write the rules to the game, but I sure as hell plan to follow them.

I'm also planning to apply early decision to Yale. This means that if I'm accepted I'm obligated to go there—and that I have to get my application done by sometime in September or October instead of December or January. I had been planning all along to apply early somewhere. After my family's trip to San Francisco last year, I was sure it would be Stanford—that is, until I saw Yale. But I knew no matter where I wanted to go, early decision was a good idea. For one thing, I was going to have to choose my top school at some point, so why not in September rather than April. Also, applying early is supposed to improve your chances of getting accepted, I guess because the school knows that you really believe you belong there. Actually, admissions officers usually say it doesn't matter, but I don't buy it. Anyway, it means that if I do get in, I'll know by December instead of April, so that's a plus.

I've got to go to wrestling in a few minutes, but I really don't feel like it. Last season drained me of almost all my love for the sport—and there wasn't that much to begin with. Everyone keeps asking me why I'm still doing it, but it's hard to answer that question since I don't exactly know why myself. Tonight I am going to an open mat session at a local high school. Basically, it's just an event where a bunch of high school wrestlers come together and wrestle for a few hours. Some of them are pretty good. Whenever I go to one, I end up wrestling for about 10 or 15 minutes and then sitting down and thinking about how I'd rather not be there.

This brings me to something that really bothers me about myself. My coaches, my parents, and adults in general have this picture of me as a superdisciplined kid who always gives things 100 percent. This is true in my classes and in football, but not in wrestling. For a long time I've thought of this lapse as a huge flaw, but now I'm not so sure. If I don't have any desire to continue the sport after high school, and if I don't really like it that much, should I really put tons of time into it for reasons that I'm unsure of?

➤

Coach Kornblut
Wrestling Coach

Josh is not a great wrestler. When I say that, I mean Josh is not a great athlete. He is an extremely conscientious, hardworking, self-disciplined individual. Some kids just don't have the type of build that's really conducive to wrestling. Josh was strong enough. He was in fabulous physical shape—better condition than almost any wrestler I've ever coached—but he just was limited in terms of physical power. So, since he was placing in some tournaments and working hard in practice, I saw that he was doing the best he could. I never had a doubt about that. As a coach, that's all you want.

I'm back. The trip took forever because traffic was pretty bad and all the way there I kept thinking about how I really didn't feel like going. But when I finally got there I actually wrestled well. Wrestling is the type of sport that can totally dictate your mood. Don't get me wrong; I'm not saying that all of a sudden I love the sport again, I'm just saying that after you wrestle well, you feel better about yourself. Anyway, I wrestled well tonight and now I'm in a pretty good mood.

Unfortunately, I've got a couple of things I need to deal with. For one, I have a slight problem with the work that I was going to do this summer with Habitat for Humanity. I need to do it for my applications, but the week that I had scheduled for it, I have football camp. I thought I would have my afternoons free to volunteer, but yesterday I was reminded that the offensive linemen have an extra session starting at six that week. It's not that big of a deal; all I have to do is call the Habitat people up and explain that I have a prior commitment—I'm sure that something can be worked out. Still, it's annoying. Also, I have to get a physical before the 15th, when the camp starts up.

I'm pretty excited about next season. I think that our team is going to be very good. It's a little weird that after this year, I'll never be on a football team again. On the one hand, it's going to be nice actually to be able to go right home after school and not to have to lift weights or work out everyday. On the other hand, football has become such a big part of my life, I'm not sure what I'll do without it.

I know that I would be a very different person if I hadn't played. I probably would be either a huge nerd or a big burnout. Football gave me a chance to meet people that I wouldn't have met otherwise. Though my high school prides itself on being integrated—which is sort of true if you just look at the numbers (the school is 50 percent black and 50 percent white) —in reality, the school is very segregated. Black kids and white kids almost never sit together at lunch or hang out after school. But the football team is different. I'm not saying that everyone on the team leaves all of their differences at the locker room door, or that the guys hug and kiss when they pass in the hall (actually, I've never seen anyone on the football team kiss some other guy, and I don't think I'm likely to see that any time soon), but the players on the team make an effort to get along, and we all have a pretty good time.

It's weird to think that a year from now I'll be getting ready to leave home for good. I'm definitely ready for high school to be over. It seems like there will be a lot less crap at college. I don't even know what crap I'm talking about exactly, but I still think that there will be less of it once I get there.

7/5/96—That's pretty much what happened—but with a few twists . . .

Last night was one of the more interesting Fourth of Julys I've had. The plan: I and two of my friends would go over to this girl Jessica's house (Jessica, a.k.a. "J") where everyone—but me, of course—would get drunk. I would drive them to the fireworks and on to a big party. That's pretty much what happened—but with a few twists. When we got to our first stop, who should be there but Emily. To begin with, I felt extremely uncomfortable with her there, after all the weirdness between us. Then they all started drinking, and within an hour Emily was acting like a complete idiot. She was being loud and obnoxious—and not all that nice—and was acting a lot more drunk than she actually could have been. I understand that when some people get loaded, they act stupid, but she was falling over herself, and the furniture, and it was the consensus among those present that she was exaggerating. She got worse in the car. She was being a bitch, yelling at people for being loud—even though the loudest person in the car was her. She didn't talk much at the fireworks (thankfully), but she complained all the way to the party. The car—a two-door Honda Civic—had eight people in it, so everyone was uncomfortable, but she was bitching about how she was cramped and how I wouldn't listen to her directions. Every time she opened her mouth, she bothered me more and more.

We got to the party, which was broken up by the police about a second after we arrived. I mean, we didn't even get to the front door. By the time we got all eight of us back in the car *and* got Emily back to her friend's house, I couldn't believe that this was the same person I've been crazy about for the past year.

I think it's because she was drinking, and she was doing it just to impress people. I don't particularly have a problem with people drinking or smoking. But people who drink or smoke just to look cool really get on my nerves. I realize that last night may have been an exception to the way Emily usually acts, but at this point I really don't care. She was being annoying at a time when I was ready to get over her, so it worked out. I don't think that my opinion of a person has ever changed so drastically over the course of one night.

Now I need to find somebody else to get interested in. I know that you can't always choose whom you like, but I'm hoping that it will be someone who won't actually want a relationship with me.

Meanwhile, the girl my friend Alex is interested in, Sharon, won't even talk to him. His situation is a bit different from mine because, unlike me, he actually had a relationship with this girl.

He is very upset about the whole thing. Girls talk a lot about how poorly guys treat them, but from my experience—and from the experience of most of my friends—girls are just as mean and conniving as guys are.

One of my dad's old college friends just called. A couple of months ago he was in town so my parents and I went out to dinner with him. The whole night was basically him and my dad talking about all of the things they did at school. Hearing them reminisce that way reminded me of how much I want to get out of college besides studying. I know that I want to go to med school after college, so I'm expecting to work at least as hard as I have in high school, which is about four to five hours a night. But I also want to have a good time.

During the school year I was talking to this friend of mine, Shellie. Shellie wants to go to Harvard, and if she doesn't get in, it will be a huge surprise to everyone. She's got perfect scores on her SATs and on all *ten* of her AP exams, is president of the debate club, and on and on and on. She also happens to be a very sweet girl, and I am always amazed that such a down-to-earth person can be so intelligent. She's one of the ten or so people my age who I have genuine respect for.

►

Shellie
Harvard-Bound Buddy

I met Josh in eighth grade. He used to make fun of me a lot. My impressions of him then were basically the same as they are now. He's funny and a little wild. He usually says what's on his mind. He was my lab partner in Chemistry last year, which was fun.

I worked hard in high school because I'm pretty clear about what I'd like to do when I get older. I'd like to be a criminal defense lawyer, and eventually I'd like to become a judge, maybe a Supreme Court Justice. I kind of do things in steps. High school was one step toward my final goal of getting into Harvard. I guess it's possible that the problem with a lot of teenagers is that they think that what they do in high school won't have consequences later on. I think that a lot of times they do, so I've always tried to keep in mind that what I do now makes a difference.

I think the primary purpose of college is to study and to learn just because it's higher education. I guess it's partially also to be social and to have fun, but that's sort of secondary. I think it's good to be focused and directed and to know what you want, but I don't think that it's good to be obsessed to the point where it like consumes your life. And in that sense, Josh is a little bit much.

Anyway, I was talking to her about school, and she said that the whole point of college was to study, but I think that's kind of stupid, and I told her so. College should be a time when you meet people and learn not only about why two plus two is four but how to get along with people who are different from you. Basically, what I'm saying is that a social life is half of a college education.

Speaking of studying too much, I went out and bought a review book for my SAT IIs earlier today. I feel a little stupid about my score because the test covered basic grammar. The book that I bought was $12, and another one was $18. It got me thinking about how much college costs. The tuition for Yale and the other Ivies is around $30,000. With the money my parents will spend on my and my sister's education, they could buy a small island in the Bahamas. These schools have about 10,000 students each. I realize that a lot of kids are on financial aid, but I assume that the majority of them have to pay it back. So what the hell do these schools do with all of that money? Maybe I'll find out once I get there, but right now, it seems like an awful lot to pay for a diploma.

My mom just walked in and told me that my dad's friend was calling to tell us that his father died. When I was five or six, I had this incredible fear of death. I'm talking about fear that keeps you awake at night. I wasn't really worried about dying—I was more afraid that once you were dead, it would be like sleeping forever. This whole episode scared the pants off my parents. I think they thought I was going to grow up all out of whack. So far I think I'm doing okay . . . although my dad thinks I'm a little weird. Anyway, I'm glad that I went through that phase when I was younger, because I never worry about it anymore.

7/6/96—I can't tell if I'm applying to college or buying a used car . . .

I've always wanted to be one of those people who went out every night and did stuff. This summer, for the first time, I'm actually doing that. And I'm finding out that it's really not that much more exciting than sitting at home watching TV. It might be better if I smoked or drank, but I don't, so I basically sit and watch *other* people smoke and drink, which is about as boring as a bad sitcom. Tonight, for instance, I went over this kid Rob's house and sat there for a few hours while he and his friends got drunk. The evening's climax was when some girls came over for some beer and pot. (Emily was there, but she hadn't had anything to drink so she wasn't acting like a complete fool. It's kind of funny that for the past year I've been trying, unsuccessfully, to figure out how to be where Emily was going to be when she went out, and now that she's getting on my nerves, I can't seem to get away from her.)

I've been getting up late in the morning or afternoon. I think I'll start getting up earlier so I can actually enjoy these few days of relaxation that I have before football practice starts.

I'm starting to get mail from colleges whose first solicitations I didn't respond to. They say that it's not too late if I act now— I can still request information! I can't tell if I'm applying for college or buying a used car from a guy named Sleazy Eddie.

7/7/96—Sometimes people are just incredibly stupid . . .

Sometimes people are just incredibly stupid. Tonight I went out to this place called the Cosmopolitan. It's a dance club that has "teen nights" every week. I've only been there once, and I don't think I'll be going back anytime soon. The kid I went with, Rob Emrich (the same guy I've been hanging out with for most of the summer), almost got in a fight. The club was pretty dull, since there was no one we really knew. Rob, who was pretty gone, started messing with kids who were smoking, busting their balls about being underage. He was just screwing around. I thought it was hilarious—imagine a 17-year-old going over to a bunch of 16-year-olds and telling them they're breaking the law. But the kids didn't think it was too funny, and they—all six of them— told him so. Before I knew what was going on, I was watching a fight break out. Some security guards came over and broke it up. Later on these kids came back with about ten of their friends, to stir things up. Rob had conveniently lost his contact lens, so I did most of the talking. Talk about hilarious—these guys were all trying to stare me down, talking about how they were going to kick our asses and how they were some hard-ass dudes who don't screw around, while Rob is scurrying around on his hands and knees going "Where's my contact? I lost my contact!" But I just kept on talking bullshit and telling them to chill out. Finally the whole thing got broken up by a security guard and we left soon after.

There were a couple of things I found interesting about the experience. First of all, it furthered my growing belief that violence is stupid. I mean, how would those guys taking my friend out back and beating the shit out of him solve anything? Second, and along those lines, it got me thinking about what adults think of teenagers, and why. More often than not, when something is said about teens on the national news, it has to do with sex, drugs, or violence. I take great offense when teens are categorized as selfish, ignorant, gun-toting alcoholics. But the thing is, kids my age seem to be intent on proving those reports right. Even I am starting to believe some of the stereotypes, though I have many friends who don't use drugs or alcohol, are incredibly intelligent, have real views on world issues, and are more mature than a lot of adults I know.

I sort of feel like I'm being a lazy son-of-a-bitch lately. All of my friends seem to be working or going on vacation. I'm not really doing anything except playing football and wrestling. I am reading a lot, going out a lot, and watching a lot of movies. But I feel guilty. I guess I wouldn't feel any better if I were bussing tables for eight hours a day or working in a lab. I would be bored and angry about not taking advantage of this last summer of my high school years. And after this week is over, I'll have stuff to do. Even if I wanted to go out during two-a-days, I don't think that I'll able to get up to go to the bathroom, let alone socialize.

I've got to start getting in shape. Today I ran four miles, and I felt like I was going to pass out. I also should wrestle more. Last night I was thinking about this one match from last year. It happened during a unusual weekend because the majority of the team—including the good wrestlers—were at another tournament, and the normal JV squad—that means me—were wrestling a dual meet. Our coach thought that this would work out because the JV guys were wrestling one of the worst high schools in the area. To make a long story short, I ended up losing, and my defeat lost us the match. It was one of the most embarrassing days of my entire life. The kid I lost to was really bad, and I know that I'm much better than he. There are tons of excuses that I could make, but the bottom line is that I lost to a terrible wrestler.

I still think about that match sometimes, like I did last night (actually, more like every single day). It absolutely killed my self-confidence, not just in wrestling but in everything. The next day I got my grades, and I had only one B (which I brought up to an A second semester). I realized that if I had put more time into wrestling and won the match, and put less time into my school-work and gotten poor grades, it would have had a much greater effect on my life. I would have no chance of getting into Yale or any of the schools I'm applying to. What I'm trying to say is that getting my grades the next day gave me some perspective on the role and importance of wrestling in my life, and some validation for the decisions I'd made about my priorities. Still, though, that match is just one of those things that sort of sticks in my head and no matter how hard I try to get it out, I can't.

But I do want to make an effort to enjoy next wrestling season, something that I have never exactly enjoyed. It may be hard, seeing that I will hear from Yale on December 15, which is right when the season begins. Oh, well. Meanwhile, Rob was the one who convinced me to go out for the team in eighth grade. Maybe I should have let those dudes kick his ass. If it was during the season, I might have even given him a shot or two myself!

▶

Coach Kornblut
Wrestling Coach

The Valley Forge match was certainly one of those types of matches where you can only shrug your shoulders. But like I said, if the kids you coach walk out there and give 100 percent, that's good enough.

And so often they don't. With Josh, it was the opposite. I knew his best effort was always out there. I never had a problem with his performance for that reason.

7/8/96—I was surprised at the Chemistry score . . .

My AP scores came today. I got a four in Chemistry and a five in U.S. History. Go, Josh! I was actually a little surprised at the Chemistry score, since my feeling after the test was that I probably would have done better had it been in Russian. Mom and Dad were happy.

The family was sort of bothering me at dinner. My parents wanted to know where I went last night, but I really didn't feel like telling them. It's funny, I've never liked telling them where I was going. I don't have any idea why that is. In any case, this started an argument over what exactly the big deal was. We both agreed it *wasn't* a big deal; therefore, they felt that I should tell them, and I felt that it was unnecessary. I ended up telling them and the whole thing seemed stupid. My dad said I was expressing my last vestiges of immaturity, which I think is a load of crap.

Then I got in an argument with my sister over food. She went to get dessert, and I've told her that I am trying to get in shape for the season. I started babbling about how nobody ever respects my wants or needs, which, now that I think about it, is ridiculous. I was just in that fighting mode. Oh, well.

7/10/96—After this week my schedule gets hectic . . .

Sometimes I think that my sister was put on this Earth to annoy me. She loves to get under my skin and, after 17 years, she's gotten quite good at it. I love her a lot, and she is usually a sweet, caring person. But at other times she is a selfish little bitch. I was arguing with my parents over a piece of pizza (food is like gold in my house), and she sat there mocking me and smiling. I felt like punching her in the face.

Actually, we get along very well most of the time. We used to fight like mortal enemies, but since she and I were both in high school at the same time, we've been getting along. I can honestly say that she is one of my best friends. Once in a while, though, we revert to our former selves and fight. When we do, it's usually because she is making fun of me, like tonight. I guess it's because I respect her opinion more than anyone else's, and it gets me so mad when she thinks I'm acting stupid.

►

Rachael Berezin
Sister

My relationship with Josh is really good. We used to bicker a lot. We both get on each other's nerves, but Josh would do it in a mean way and I didn't. When he's mad I'll just annoy him. Like, physically. Poke him and stuff. But when I'm really upset he'll tease me and make me more upset. He's a nice guy, but he can be a real asshole.

I'm very anxious right now. After this week my schedule gets hectic. I'll have football in the mornings and evenings next week, and Habitat for Humanity in between. Then I have one more week of lifting before practice starts. That's the rest of my summer. So instead of relaxing and enjoying these last couple weeks, I'm spending them worrying.

Tomorrow the football team is going to the Metzenbaum Center, a place for mentally retarded children. I think that this trip will be really good for me and the rest of the team. It's always good to get some perspective, and I'm sure that this will give me and the guys a healthy dose.

7/14/96—He must have some serious brain damage . . .

I had a good time on our trip to the Metzenbaum Center on Thursday. We played baseball, ate, and participated in a talent show with the kids. I even danced . . . and got a lot of crap from everybody for not having any rhythm. It's on tape, but I don't dare watch it. I have a feeling that it may come back to haunt me when the highlight film comes out.

I didn't go out on Thursday or Friday night. I sat home, watched movies, and read. I saw *Platoon* for the first time. My parents wouldn't let me watch it when it first came out, and I remember being really upset about that. After seeing it now, I think they made the right call.

On Saturday, the football team held a car wash. Car washes are the most boring things I have ever done. You'll clean maybe twenty cars, think that you're almost done, and then realize it's only 11:30 and the car wash ends at 3. Thankfully, I only have to do that one more time.

Oh yeah, I also had my last sports physical on Thursday. I know that's not the most momentous occasion in the world, but it made me realize that I'm starting to think of everything I do— car washes, physicals, and the like—in terms of it being the last time.

Anyway, Saturday night I went down to Massilon, Ohio, with a bunch of guys on the team to watch a football all-star game. (An all-star game is a game between two all-star teams made up of the best high school players in the area. I don't know who picks the teams, though . . . the football gods?) A tailback, Shawn Wright, played in it from Shaker. I've never been on the sidelines while he's been running, and I realized just how good he is. The other kids he was playing with were big, fast, and strong. I'm talking six foot five inches and 275 pounds big. Shawn was involved in two touchdowns and got the MVP award. It was a good time, even though I almost got in an accident on the way home.

Today I woke up early, ten o'clock. I watched *This Week with David Brinkley*, which (along with *Capital Gang* and *60 Minutes*) is a show that I don't feel guilty about watching. I used to watch seven or eight hours of TV a day, but for the past couple of years I'm down to two or three max.

Then I went to the orientation for Habitat for Humanity. It was in a terrible neighborhood, no more than 15 minutes away from the disgustingly huge houses I pass on my way to school, which really makes you think. Today's meeting made me realize that this might end up being more than something for my applications—it could turn out to be a really great experience, although I can tell already I'll be totally exhausted by each day's end.

7/18/96—The complexity of the situation . . .

Okay, for the past four days I've been running from football to the ghetto and back again. As soon as I got to the site on my first day of Habitat work, some guy came up to me and said, "We're going to run all over you." He turned out to be another high school kid who's on one of the teams on our school's football schedule (Lakewood) and was trying to talk junk to me. I'll be glad to respond after we win, but until then I'll keep my mouth shut. Anyway, besides all that, I went right to work, shoveling gravel. I did this for a few hours. Everyone seemed nice, except for the kid from Lakewood.

The next couple of days were less eventful. I would do something for an hour or two and then sit on my butt waiting for directions for another two hours. The most exciting moment was when I got called a "white bitch" by some kid on a bike. He even punched me in the shoulder. I figured I wasn't in the right place to get in a racially motivated fight—it could have started a riot. Also there were these three ladies, working for Habitat, who had no understanding of where they were or the complexity of the situation. They kept waving cheerfully to kids who walked by on the street. That is, they did until one of the kids responded with "I'm all right, baby, but I'd be better if you would come over here and. . ." Aside from that, everyone in the neighborhood was quite amiable.

7/21/96—I can't remember a more rewarding experience . . .

I have been shoveling dirt for the past three days. I met the lady who is moving into one of the Habitat for Humanity houses. She is a truly kind person and just generally very cool. I wonder how she got herself into the position of needing a Habitat home. I like working here so much that I am coming back for another week. Hopefully they'll let me use more power tools. Men with power tools are a funny bunch. A guy could never have been within a mile of a construction site, but put a drill in his hands, and he knows more than Bob Vila.

Actually, this might even be a good thing to write a college essay on. Habitat for Humanity, I mean, not men with power tools. People who work in admissions say that you should start your essays in the summer, but it's hard since the same admissions people don't give you the topics until the fall. In any case, it could be a problem writing an "original essay" on a subject like volunteer work. I can just see the readers' eyes rolling as they read

"I learned a lot about building homes, but even more about how good it feels to help those in need." Gag.

Today my sister told me that I have no tact. First of all, I don't agree with her assessment. Second, tact is nothing more than lying and false sympathy. If you really care about someone, you don't need to censor what you say to them. That way, when you tell them something, good or bad, they know that there's no BS.

I went out on Friday night, but instead of being with my usual football and school buddies, it was with a real live girl, Kate. Okay, so maybe one or two of my football pals tagged along, but it was still the closest thing to a date I've had in a while.

7/22/96—He's a funny kid . . .

Today I saw this guy from my Chemistry class, Matt, in the weight room. He's a funny kid. Everyone thinks he is one of the hardest-working people in the school just because he's second in the class. He's got them fooled pretty well. He does less work than anyone I know.

In any case, he asked if I had gotten any applications yet. He hadn't, either. It seems to me that colleges ought to send out schedules or, at the very least, tell you if and when they are going to send you an application. The few colleges that do are the ones that I have absolutely no interest in. I keep getting letters from small Ohio schools asking me if I've forgotten about them. One of these days I'm going to write back and tell them I am *trying* to forget about them as much as possible, but it is difficult when they keep on sending me letters. I think maybe I should call up the schools I am interested in and request an application. (Now there's a bright idea.)

Also, one of my best friends, Aaron, got home today from an

away wrestling tournament. He and I are the exact same person—except he's six foot two, 250 pounds, African-American, and he actually *enjoys* wrestling. Other than that, we really are the same.

It's strange, I can't really think of how to describe him, I guess because we're such good friends. I always hang out with him during football and wrestling practices, and I even wrestled him once last year. Boy, was that a bad idea. He outweighs me by about 70 pounds, and he made me see stars (literally). I can only remember being mad at Aaron one time, and that was in football. He kept blocking the person I was supposed to block, and I lost it. I just started shouting out the name of the play, "47 Z Outside! That's my man! 47 Z Outside," with my face all bright red, totally freaking out. Ah, the good old days.

Like I said, he's a lot like me. He's sarcastic 90 percent of the time, but he knows how and when to focus. And his luck with women is roughly the same as mine. We always talk about how much easier it would be if we were mean. Girls seem to like guys who treat them like crap. He also has had the wonderful experience of having girls come up and hug him all the time, like he's some huge teddy bear, and then look really surprised (or, worse, laugh out loud) when he asks if they're interested. I tell Aaron as much about myself as I tell anyone.

I've come to the conclusion that I shouldn't let wrestling depress me. I made the choice, a while ago, that I wasn't willing to put tons of time into a sport that did not bring me tons of enjoyment. Now I just have to accept that this means I won't be incredibly successful when it comes to winning matches.

I don't think I'll go to Habitat today. It is already 3:15 and I want to work out later. I plan to go the rest of the week, though. That's the only problem with not going today—I might be more likely not to go tomorrow or the next day. I am an extremely disciplined person, but once I get into (or out of) the habit of doing something, I get stuck. This pattern worked well for me during the school year. I got into the habit of going to the library to study, and I ended up doing it every day. When I was a freshman, though, I would miss one day of wrestling (in the off season, of course) and that would be it for a good three weeks. I think now I'm starting to find some middle ground—I can take a day off, not feel guilty about it, and come back the next day. This approach, though, doesn't really apply to football, school, or in-season wrestling, for that matter. I haven't missed a football or wrestling practice all year, and I've never even been late to a football practice through three years of high school. What I do have a problem with is stuff like cleaning my room or paying parking tickets (of which I have two outstanding). This is an aspect of my life that I know I have to work on.

I'm not so worried about it now, but once I'm living alone, without my parents as a safety net, these little things could become big problems. My room, speaking of problems, is the messiest it has ever been. Generally, there's no gross stuff like old food (although I did find a fork, and when I went to pick it up, found it was glued to a plate by old macaroni and cheese), but every letter or handout I received last year is currently on my floor. Maybe that would be a good project to start today. I'll work slowly so as not to shock my mother into a stupor.

7/23/96—I have a terribly annoying conscience . . .

I have a problem with parked cars. The week after I got my license, I hit a pole in our parking garage. One week later I hit a parked car across from our apartment building while trying to pull out of a space. Then, on Homecoming night, I hit yet another parked car. The "accidents"—if you call hitting immobile objects at a slow speed accidents—cost me about $1,200. My luck seems not to be changing . . . I just bumped into *another* parked car after dropping off a friend. This time I did not leave a note, as I have in the past. I feel bad about it, but there's nothing I can do now.

The thing is, I have a terribly annoying conscience. I even told my parents about my latest high-speed crash. I can never do anything bad without feeling terrible about it. After telling my parents, I usually feel better, but that doesn't change the fact that it would often be a lot easier if I could be dishonest.

For instance, there have been times when I've *almost* cheated on tests. After I'm done filling in my answers, once in a very long while I'll look at someone else's paper, just to see what they thought about number 57. And occasionally I see that I have the wrong answer, go back and do the problem again, and find that I just made a silly mistake the first time. So I change the answer. But every single time I do this, I change it back. I've never turned in a test that reflected anyone's work but my own. And last year I found that I could spare myself the whole agonizing process simply by not looking at other people's answers in the first place.

I did go to Habitat today, but there was no one working the afternoon shift, so I went home. I'm glad that I gave it a shot though.

7/24/96—He has no business talking about gymnastics . . .

Well, the '96 Olympics are here. The Olympics are the coolest thing ever, except for John Tesh. I liked him on *Entertainment Tonight*, but he has no business talking about gymnastics. The other night he wouldn't let five minutes go by without reminding you that the music you heard was from a competitor's floor exercise. And I thought that they were just playing it to keep the crowd amused.

There are a few things I need to take care of before the year starts. My room and my applications, for instance, although not necessarily in that order. (Where *is* that Yale application???) Besides those two things, I also need to set some goals for the year. My football coach talks about goal-setting constantly, and it has been extremely helpful to me. The main thing I need to figure out is how well I want to do in my classes first semester. I know that I can get the grades I want, but I have to look at the decision from a mental health perspective. If I want to get all As, I'll have to study as hard as, if not harder than, last year, and last year was no fun. I'm sure that I'll make getting straight As a goal, but I think it is worth a little thought before I make that commitment.

7/25/96—Another thing I won't miss are the car washes . . .

Today was my last off-season lift and my last organized running workout. Believe it or not, I'm not too depressed about the passing of this era. For one thing, it's really hard work. I mean, running is probably not even the right word for those torture sessions. They actually involve plyometrics (jumping and bounding and hopping to build power in the legs) and sprinting, both of which are tremendously tiring. For another, I'll be doing plenty of running and lifting during wrestling season. Still, I've participated in countless off-season workouts over the past three years, and it is strange to imagine life without them. Another thing I won't miss are the car washes. Saturday is my last one. Thank God. I'm ready for this summer to be over with and to get going with football. But at the same time, I wish I could have a few more months off.

7/26/96—I assume that he was inebriated . . .

Well, yet another interesting night in a summer full of interesting nights. I was supposed to go over to Jessica's house and then somewhere else from there, all of which is pretty par for the course, but our plans got screwed up. The people I was with didn't want to go, and, to be quite honest, I was a bit of a pushover. In any case, I ended up driving a bunch of drunk people around all night. The evening ended when one of the drunkards in my car suddenly felt it was necessary to yell out the window at someone we passed—on the street where one of my friends needed to be dropped off. The kid who'd been yelled at chased after us and, when he caught up, threw a bottle at the car. I assume he was, like my friends, inebriated.

I still haven't had one time when I've left the house and not had to think about college. It was part of the conversation all last night. Actually, the bulk of the talk was about how odd it is that we'll be seniors. I don't really know how to feel about that. On one hand, I want to get it all over with (by "it" I mean football, wrestling, high school, getting in to college—everything), but on the other, I want to have an enjoyable senior year. Somehow I don't think I can have both, but you never know. In one more week, it will all start and I'll be so busy doing it I won't have to worry about it anymore.

Part Two

▶

Apply
Yourself

*7/29/96—The first thing I noticed was that it
was long . . .*

The wait is over. Well, not really, but I got an application from
Columbia today. It came with a 50-page booklet filled with
famous alumni (they even threw in Jack Kerouac, who's more
known for dropping out of Columbia than going there),
extolling the virtues of a New York City education. I've read that
type of pamphlet before, although this one was bigger and better than most others. Even so, it was the same old stuff, except in
the middle of all of this bullshit was an application.

The first thing that I noticed about the application was that
it was long . . . about 23 pages long. The first page was instruc-
tive, and following the dictates of my masculinity, I skipped it.
The next thing that caught my eye was a letter from the

Columbia Office of Undergraduate Admissions. The letter is actually quite reassuring. It starts off rather inauspiciously, saying they know that the process is nerve-racking at least and that this stress "may prompt from me safe responses and safe choices." It goes on to say that by applying to Columbia, I am taking a risk. But, they advise, I should know I have worked hard and should try to enjoy the self-examination the admissions process evokes. By the end of the letter, I have been assured that my application will be looked over carefully and they will try to make the right choice. They should add that when it gets down to the wire, they resort to throwing applications down the steps and seeing which one gets to the floor first. Seriously, though, they really seem to be trying to make me feel at ease about the application process. The flip side of the letter has Columbia College Major Codes, SEAS (School of Engineering and Applied Science) Major Codes, and Extracurricular Activity Codes—what they are codes *for* I'm not really sure, but I'm guessing I will eventually have to use them on the application.

Section One of the application is next, appropriately titled: "Application for Admission I," where they tell me to be sure to read the directions before I start. (By the way, at this point I intentionally don't have a writing utensil within 50 feet of my person, since I know I'll need to practice writing out my name and address at *least* three times, to make sure I get it right. So skipping over the directions now poses no real threat.) Section One is divided into smaller subsections: "Personal Data" (Name, Address, Phone #, etc.); "Application Data" (Probable Major, how I heard about Columbia, Campus Visit or not, etc.); "Secondary Schools"; "Citizenship"; "Optional" (where they ask me to "describe myself as a member of one of these groups." I'll have to ask my parents if they're sure that our families are from Russia and Poland, because Jewish is apparently not one of "these groups"). Finally, they ask us to choose three probable extracurricular activities. All in all, pretty simple.

The next section is titled "Application for Admission II," and it also asks for my name and address (I'm getting the feeling I'm going to have to read those directions at some point) and is concerned with my family—who they are, what they do, where they went/are going to school, and things of that nature. No potential weaknesses yet, assuming I can spell my name correctly (which, at this point, is questionable). But turn the page, and there they are: "College Entrance Exams." SATs, no problem. SAT IIs are a little more troublesome. They want three scores: writing and two others. The other two aren't an issue, but that pesky 660 is still bothering me. Now the directions are a must; I need to find out when the submission deadline is so I know if I need to send my new score separate from my application. I'm sure it's a simple procedure; all I have to do is get an 800 on the test, and I'll be fine.

Now they ask me where I go to school (*again*) and several questions about language. I think I'll be able say I'm fluent in Spanish by the time I turn in the application. I've heard that being proficient in a second language is a big plus at Columbia. (Mostly from my dad. While planning my summers, he would always suggest doing something that incorporated community service and Spanish. He bugged me about this until I got so mad I almost exploded. Then he did it a few more times.) They also ask about my disciplinary record—there should be no problems there, unless they count parking tickets.

Then it gets rough again. There are three lines for "honors and prizes you have been awarded since the sophomore year." The only award I've gotten is a certificate from Purdue, that basically says that I was the best Social Studies student in my class. This means there will be plenty of blank space, and it seems to me that blank space is the enemy on college applications. Next are five lines for "School-related activities." I sure as hell hope I can put football and wrestling down there, or else I'm in bad shape. Fortunately, they do provide ten lines to explain which activity is most important and why. If I can express how much football has meant to me in those ten lines, it should make up for the blank space on the rest of the page.

Section Three, the "Application for Financial Aid," surprisingly, asks for *my* wages and income, and how much money I have in the bank. Yeah, I'm a regular mogul.

By the looks of the next section, I'll need to get all As one last time: the "Mid-Year School Report." My guidance counselor fills out the "Secondary School Report," another in this litany of evaluations. Hopefully this will be the one that gets me in. *Again* they want my name and stuff. (The fact that you send in all of the sections separately would explain the redundancy of the application in this aspect.) They ask for nine things on this section: (1) Class Rank and GPA; (2) Test Scores; (3) General Ratings, a chart my guidance counselor is supposed to fill out (for some reason they don't at my high school), rating me Average or Below, Good, Excellent, Outstanding, or "One of the top few I have ever encountered in my career," in each of 16 areas ranging from Academic Creativity, to Reaction to Setbacks. (I think Mrs. Blattner will rate me well. You know, explaining this feels like trying to explain the scoring for Olympic Gymnastics. Now all I need are some commentators saying "Ooohhh, that's a shame, he was having such a great routine, now he won't be a factor for a medal," whenever I screw up.) (4) Suspensions and Expulsions; (5) Senior Year Classes; (6) School Community Service Requirement and whether I have met it, not met it, or "significantly exceeded it" (our school has no requirement, but I think I have done about 75 hours by now); (7) Curriculum

Difficulty, on a scale of Average or Below, Somewhat Demanding, Demanding, or Very Demanding—I'll throw a fit if I find out she doesn't say Very Demanding; (8) Class Comparison, how I compare to my entire class in terms of academics, character, and overall achievement (I have a real strong class academically, so this could be another problem spot); and finally, (9) a Summary Report.

The last two sections are teacher recommendations. Basically they ask teachers the same questions as they do the guidance counselor, but ask for a longer essay. I know the one from Mr. Pollack, my eleventh-grade history teacher, will be stellar, but the other is up in the air.

I thought I had gotten through the application without having to write an essay, but no such luck. Section Two continues after the recommendation forms (that's right, *after* Section Four—go figure), and they ask for outside activities. Here comes my volunteer work and my Outward Bound experience. If I write this paragraph well, it could be a real strong point; if not, it will look like all I do is sit around and watch *The Simpsons*. (Well, it's not *all* I do.) They want to know what I did over the last two summers, what books I've read and enjoyed in the past year (I'm glad now that I've done some outside reading. I think I should continue to do that), list the newspapers and magazines I read regularly, list the films I've enjoyed, and explain how I became interested in Columbia. After that, all I need to do is write a killer essay. (That might be the key on all of these applications.) That's the whole thing! I need to look it over a few more times, make some copies, and go over it with my guidance counselor. I always worry I won't look good on paper, but I might be able to sell myself quite well. I don't understand how they can reach fair decisions about who gets in, but at least after reading this, I think I have as good a shot as anyone.

8/1/96—I never thought it would be so hard to figure out who I am . . .

August's here. That's bad. Two-a-days start a week from yesterday and go until the beginning of September. This is about as hard as football gets. They're called two-a-days because we literally practice twice a day—and that's not even counting meetings and lifting. I'm actually excited about them this year, although I know they'll be tough. I think that if one was *forced* to do this kind of routine, it would be considered abuse. In fact, I bet that if a prisoner was forced to do the kind of work we did, he would sue the jail.

►

Coach Sedmak
Football Coach

I look at two-a-days as a real mild form of boot camp. They basically spend the entire month of August training, when it's hot—80 to 85 degrees. Their summer's over. We don't give them much time to do anything else. They wake up in the morning and they're tired and they're sore and they have to go and do it again, two or three times. I told the kids, for some of you, it will be the hardest thing you ever do.

I'm a little concerned about this year's team. Some of the seniors are starting to argue, and we need to be coming together now, not falling apart at the seams. But a few of the guys are starting to step up as leaders, and I think that the team will gel once we get going. One more month until we play St. Ed's, one of the best teams in the area (which makes them one of the best in the state because northeast Ohio has really good high school football).

I read the application to Columbia over a few times and had my dad make copies of it for me. I filled one out as practice, and as I did I realized the essay is where I can highlight some things I have done over the past four years. There is no place on the application where I can write down my experiences with Outward Bound, so that could be an essay topic.

Outward Bound was really incredible. I heard about it from a friend of mine freshman year who had the brochures. I'd always wanted to go camping, and it looked like a really cool program. They have four mottoes—service, physical fitness . . . and two others I can't remember right now—so the program combines camping and community service, which was perfect for me. I did it the summer after freshman year (before I was so crazy about football that I couldn't miss a couple weeks).

From the start it was exciting. I left my parents in Cleveland and flew to Ashville, North Carolina. The day I arrived, my group (there were ten kids and a leader in each group) got in a van and drove out to a trail into the mountains. We camped out in the woods that night (under a tarp, not a tent) and spent the first five days of the program backpacking. Then there was a three-day canoe trip before our first community service duty, which was to help paint a homeless shelter downtown. (The food we had at the homeless shelter was, by far, the best food we had on the whole trip. And we got to sleep inside for once.) After three days of rock-climbing we did our second service project, helping this guy deliver firewood to very low income families in rural North Carolina who don't have heat in their houses. (I'm talking *Deliverance* backwoods here.) That was pretty cool. The final expedition was a three-day solo trip. We were each given one bagel, a hunk of cheese, a little bag of dates and a little bag of nuts, and sent out on our own. The first night was really scary (and really wet—it storms a lot in North Carolina, I kept sliding out from under my tarp), but really great, too. The whole experience really fit in with all the discipline and leadership work I've done for football. It teaches you how to work with a group and be a good leader, and I value that.

So what I would really like to do is tie in Outward Bound with some of my other activities. That won't be too hard. For instance, I could talk about how doing community service work through that program got me interested in volunteering. The only problem is it wouldn't be very exciting or unique.

I know the whole point of keeping this journal is that it would make a great essay, but since I only have one shot for Columbia, I think maybe it's more important to talk about the things I've done during my high school career and save my secret weapon for Yale. Most colleges give you an opportunity to write two essays, and some schools, like Penn, actually ask you specific questions. I figure that when I am writing two (which will hopefully be the case for Yale), I can write one essay about something like football and another about something more abstract.

I wish people hadn't drilled the idea into my head that you need a unique essay. I should just write about the effect football has had on my life. That would be genuine, *and* give an accurate impression of what I'm all about. But no, apparently that would be boring and unoriginal, so I have to write about how I sit and watch bees, and contemplate where they have been all day and all of the interesting people they've encountered. I guess I could write an essay to that effect, and it wouldn't be completely inaccurate. I mean, sometimes I do sit and think about what the stranger sitting next to me is thinking, or think about world issues, but that doesn't really represent who I am. (Or maybe it does?) I never thought it would be so hard to figure out who I am and what I'm about, and then relate it in the space provided.

It's annoying that Columbia only gives two forms for teacher recommendations. I need one from my football coach. His will help me tremendously, largely because he knows me better than my teachers do. He also can explain that football was not just something I did so I could date cheerleaders. (Even if I had, it sure didn't work too well.) He knows I've really dedicated four years of my life to him and the team. I'm sure there is some way to get an extra form or to have him write a letter. I'll need to call and ask.

That's another funny thing: I called a few colleges the other day to ask for applications, and I felt like I needed to be on top of my game. I'm sure I was talking to some secretary who has nothing to do with the admissions process, but after I hung up, I was mad at myself for acting so stupid (i.e., not knowing the year I was going to enter college). Maybe they tape these conversations and they become the deciding factor when the committee members can't make up their minds. If a request for an application went so poorly, I can't wait to see how my interview will go!

►

Tamara Shirdak
Yale Admissions Officer

There have been some interesting things that come in to us. Someone sent us a shoe and said, "Now I have one foot in the door." I've read essays that have made me sit back and say "I don't know if I'll ever write that well," or "That is an amazing self-awareness for a 17-year-old to have." I've read teacher recommendations and gotten really excited about a student, knowing the teacher has worked hard to put this student on paper and they've done it. Or sometimes I read about a student who has done something academically and it's just so impressive that it stands out to me. I have to sort of sit back and say that we're lucky that student is applying to Yale.

8/4/96—Bed is sounding good . . .

This is starting to be a bit overwhelming. So much is going to be happening in the next eight or nine months, and I'm not sure if I am ready for it. I've been thinking about it all summer, and these past few days especially, but it still seems like the beginning of the year snuck up on me. I still have so much to do, so many more hours to waste, so much of my brain to rot in front of the tube. I also have yet to clean my room, though I did get started on it yesterday. My general strategy is to go from one end of the room to the other, like five or six times, and put stuff in different containers—stuff I need to keep, stuff I need to throw out, stuff I need to go through. Usually I only get as far as the boxes, and then when I need to find something I just dump the box out. Yesterday I picked up the clothes and put them in a bag and then got distracted. Also on my to-do list for the last two days of vacation: finish reading *The Autobiography of Malcolm X*, set goals for football season and the rest of the year, and relax.

Actually, I'm not as nervous about football as I have been in the past couple of years. I know exactly what to expect. I am, however, worried about wrestling. I have no idea how to set realistic goals for myself. I can put those concerns on the back burner for a while, though, seeing that wrestling is not for another four months.

The Olympics ended tonight and that got me thinking. Here are these amazing athletes, some of whom have devoted years of their lives to compete in the Olympics. After their Olympic careers are over—when they're too old to compete, injured, worn out—what do they do with themselves? Some of them, obnoxious basketball players from the U.S. in particular, go on to make millions of dollars. Most of them, though, must wake up the next morning and not know what to do with themselves. This scenario raised a few questions for me. First of all, what am I going to do when football and wrestling are over? I don't pretend that I have devoted as much time to athletics as Olympians do, but the comparison makes sense in my mind. What am I going to do next August, when there aren't those nasty two-a-days for me to think about? Well, I thought to myself, I'll have college to look forward to. That got me thinking again: My big, overall goals, even more than my football goals, were to go to college and medical school. Only in the past few months has the former become specific to Yale. In any case, after I finish school, what next? I don't want life after college to be a big letdown for me.

I definitely need to find a way to get rid of these negative thoughts before school starts. Negative thinking pretty much ruined my junior year, and I don't want a repeat of that episode.

Meanwhile, Columbia is still the only application I've received. I am sure Yale's will come someday when it is 1000° outside, and my only goal in life will be to raise the fork to my mouth so I can eat and then somehow make my way into bed.

Bed is sounding good right about now. I really want to sleep in tomorrow, but I think I'm going to try to get up at around nine. After all, tomorrow's the second to last day of my vacation, and I don't want to spend it sleeping.

8/6/96—I've never been more ready . . .

The first meeting of the 1996 football season has officially taken place. Two-a-days start tomorrow. I've never been more ready. For the last two years I haven't been able to sleep before the first day of practice because I was too nervous. Tonight I can't sleep because I'm too excited. I can't explain why, but I have a good feeling about this season and the year in general. Anyway, I've got to make out my list of goals and a daily schedule and make copies for my room, my car, and my locker. My goals (for the football season, and August in particular):

1. Win the Lake Erie League.
2. Go 10–0.
3. Be state champions.

Josh, these are your overall goals, the ones that you never lose sight of, and the ones that motivate you. But you have to focus on the near future, so here are your goals for two-a-days:

1. Attend all two-a-day practices, on time.
2. Be supportive of all of your teammates.
3. Say at least one encouraging thing to all of the offensive linemen every day.
4. Push the sophomores, and help them learn how the program works.
5. Hustle.
6. Run to all drills, run up to the line of scrimmage.
7. Be first in every sprint that you run.
8. Block until the whistle on every play.

Your Schedule Until School Begins (subject to change)

7:00 Wake up.
7:05 Shower.
7:20 Get dressed.
7:25 Eat a large breakfast.
7:45 Relax and digest.
8:00 Leave the house to pick up Clinton and Aaron. (Clinton is

my "little brother" on the football team, though I haven't really done anything brotherly except drive him to practice every morning.)

8:30–6:00 Practice.

6:30 (somewhere around there) Get home, eat dinner.

7:00 Read (half-hour Spanish, half-hour whatever else).

8:00 Read for pleasure.

8:30 Write in journal.

9:15 Work on SAT II workbook.

9:45 Work on applications.

10:15 Get ready for bed, and set out clothes for tomorrow.

10:30 Go to bed.

8/7/96—Nothing like a good lungful of smog . . .

Today was the first day of practice, and I'm still alive . . . I think. I didn't fall asleep until around 1 A.M. last night (I couldn't stop thinking about all the stuff that's going to happen this year), but I must have slept well because I woke up this morning ready to go. Everyone else on the team seemed equally enthused about the season. In fact, everything was going great until the last half hour or so, when it all fell apart. The guys just lost their intensity and stopped hustling. Coach yelled at us pretty bad. The thing is, the exercises weren't even that hard. The linemen got yelled at the most because most of them were out of shape. Last year we had a similar situation; we had a bad afternoon practice. We let it get to us, and our two-a-days didn't go well from that point on. Based on that, I think that a lot is going to ride on how everyone reacts to today's scolding in practice tomorrow.

Part of me is a little disgusted at the guys who were dying out there. They knew what to expect of the first practice, yet they did very little to prepare for it. I still believe we can achieve all of our goals but we're going to have to start going balls to the wall, and *soon*.

Well, my schedule pretty much went to pot. The main issue was that I got home later and had meant to wake up earlier, which clearly wasn't going to work. Two-a-days have a way of sucking away all your motivation. (Oh yeah, there was an ozone warning—there was a lot of smog *and* it was really hot—today, so everyone's lungs were burning after practice. That was fun. Next time I think I'll just tie a Styrofoam cup around my nose and try to set it on fire. Nothing like a good lungful of smog to get you ready to face the day.)

I did do some reading, but I didn't read any of my Spanish. I can't believe that my Spanish teacher gave us homework over winter break. I mean, summer break. I think it's past my bedtime. Anyway, I didn't do that reading, or any other reading, *or* finish cleaning my room. I didn't work on my application, either, although the only thing that I really can do right now is write the essay, which I don't feel like doing. I think I will revise my schedule to include a half hour of work on my essay every night, rather than my application in general. Still trying to think of a rock-'em-sock-'em-get-me-in topic for the Columbia essay, but no luck yet. My gut feeling is to write about athletics, and last year I pledged that I would listen to my gut—at least when it wasn't asking me for cookies or other junk food. But Outward Bound also seems like a good topic. I was working on cleaning out my room and got to the area of the floor that hadn't been touched for three years, and I found tons of stuff from Outward Bound, including my journal. Maybe it would be interesting to compare the goals that I set for myself in the journal from that summer with things that I actually have achieved since then. Hey, that's not a bad idea. I think I'll try it and see what happens.

I got my schedule for school next year. It looks pretty crappy.

8/8/96—Some other meltable treat . . .

Today was a bit cooler outside, so the workout wasn't as hard on people and practice went much better. We lifted in between the morning and afternoon sessions, though, so my legs feel like Jell-O. Coach Sedmak said that he had planned a lot of the yelling he did. He was pissed off that some of the larger gentlemen on the team weren't in better shape. One of the sophomores remarked that he'd never seen Coach so mad; I told him he should just wait. Coach Sedmak is probably one of the best high school football coaches in the country, and he's had more of a positive influence on my life than anyone except my family. My respect for him is immeasurable. That said, I must mention that he can get very angry sometimes, which can be unpleasant. But everyone worked a little harder today, practice was crisper, and he was happier.

►

Coach Sedmak
Football Coach

We're really tough on the kids. I've been known to have my two or three tantrums every year, and they're kind of legendary. But kids don't quit when I do that. It's like down deep they know that I really care about them and I really, truly want them to be as good as they can be. I think they appreciate that.

When I got home, I actually had a lot of energy, but I made the cardinal error of sitting down and watching TV. My night ended right there. I guess I'll just have to try those goals again tomorrow. I don't want the applications to pile up, though I guess right now that's unlikely since I only have one. But I should get started on the essays, so they're ready and waiting. I'm still confident that I can work on them and keep this journal project throughout two-a-days, though I've given myself no reason to be. I'm not worried about my laziness at home carrying over to the school year, either. For one thing, regular season practices are easier, and I go to the library right after, so I can work without the distractions of home. Hey, maybe that's not such a bad idea for two-a-days . . . although there is the matter of dinner. I could eat at the shopping center across the street from the library, I guess. Almost sounds like a plan. If I can spend a half hour on my applications and a half hour on reading a night, I should be in good shape. The alternative is not to turn on the TV until after I've accomplished something. I'm awake right now, so I might as well do some reading. Hopefully, it will put me to sleep. I'm exhausted, and my legs have gone from Jell-O to pudding. Better get some rest before they move on to ice cream or some other meltable treat.

8/12/96—I stopped when my eyes started to close . . .

Today's practice was tough. It was the first one with full pads on, and everything seemed to be moving in slow motion. I never really woke up, and I can't wait to go to bed. I always forget how much those damn pads weigh and what a huge effect they have on performance. Practice was not only long and hard (at least it wasn't hot), it was frustrating—I got moved off first-team defense. I'm not terribly upset—I'm a much better offensive player than defensive—but I like being on the field. Our first game is in three weeks. St. Ed's. If we win, this will be the biggest victory in Shaker football history. The background here is that in the early '80s, Shaker had a really great team that went undefeated until they lost to St. Ed's in the playoffs. After that loss, our team went downhill—until Coach Sedmak came along. We've been getting better every year, and a win against St. Ed's this year would reestablish us as a powerhouse outside of our league. The thought of beating them keeps me going on days like today.

After a grueling practice, I was greeted at home by another grueling application; Yale's, as a matter of fact. I'm too exhausted right now to decide if I am elated or petrified by its arrival. I read through most of the bulletin, but I stopped when my eyes started to close. Nothing new there. I didn't get around to reading through the application, although I did notice that they recommend sending the application in by October 15 for early-decision candidates. Time is running out, I've got to get cracking. I'll read it and fill in all of the fill-in-the-blank-type info tomorrow.

8/13/96—One activity's effect . . .

I read Yale's application last night before I went to bed (a sure way to get nightmares). It seems simpler than Columbia's, but it has two essays, as I hoped it would. One of them asks you to explain one activity's effect on your life. I'm not too worried about that topic, seeing that the majority of my free time in high school was (is) centered around football. The other question is very open-ended, a perfect opening for me to execute my plan. I should try to procure an application from Michigan, so that I can apply there in the early fall. (They have rolling admissions, so I'm applying there as soon as possible so that—assuming I'll be accepted—I can be in at least one school for sure.) I've *got* to do more work on my applications—these goals and schedules just don't seem to be cutting it.

8/14/96—I think I'm on edge because of two-a-days, applications, and the Republican National Convention . . .

Practice went well today, even though it was hot and muggy. Still haven't worked on applications. It's amazing how quickly 7 P.M. (when I get home) turns into 10 P.M. (the time right now). Got to get cracking. But the thing is, besides the essay, everything on Yale's application is pretty easy to fill in. Columbia's has more short-answer questions so it may take longer. The deadline on that is not until November, though, so I'm in good shape. After tomorrow morning's practice, two-a-days will be half over. They're even harder than I remembered, but I just keep reminding myself that this is the last of it—ever.

Got in a minor argument with Dad. He wanted me to let my sister use the car tomorrow, but I *absolutely* need it the *entire* day. Anyway, he barely even looked at me, let alone listened as I tried to explain that I can't give up the car on Mondays or Thursdays, because I have lifting in between practices and need the car to get lunch. I got mad that he wasn't paying any attention and I started flipping out. I think I'm on edge because of two-a-days, applications, and the Republican National Convention. The people they have speaking at that thing are mind-numbingly boring, not to mention ideologically unsound. Meanwhile, the part of my brain that hasn't been put to sleep is chanting Yale, Yale, Yale, I have to work on Yale. I really should just set aside a certain period of time each night, just half an hour or so. (I did that on my ill-fated schedule—I should have known schedules don't work during two-a-days.)

8/18/96—At my age, who knows?

On Friday afternoon Coach had a meeting with all of the seniors, where he announced the captains. Actually he announced that, at present, he wasn't naming any captains. Rather, since our class was so uniformly strong, he considered *all* of the seniors captains. I think that's a great idea. It gives everyone a greater sense of responsibility for the success of the team. Also in that meeting he said he thought we could win the state title. We know from prior experience that Coach Sedmak doesn't screw around, so a statement like that was a big confidence booster. Saturday morning was our first scrimmage. It went fairly well, but at the same time, I realized that the team (myself included) was going to have to work incredibly hard this season, and next week in particular. The last week of two-a-days is usually a good test of a team's potential for success. It is my last week of this hellish schedule (thank God), so I might as well go all out.

I received the Brown application this weekend. This particular application creates a bit of anxiety for me. I'm pretty sure that if I apply to Brown early, I'll get in. I know that's a bold statement. The only reason I say so is because Brown admits a large percentage of early-decision candidates. Even if it isn't a lock, I think my chances would be better at Brown than at Yale. Or maybe it's just that after reading Yale's bulletin, I started having these nasty little thoughts . . . I think they're called doubts. What if I'm rushing into this decision about applying early to Yale? After all, I could have been having a huge hormonal surge the weekend I was in New Haven. At my age, who knows? It would be a shame to commit myself to Yale—especially if I don't get in—*and* lose my only chance of a spot at Brown just because of a pubescent high. But I don't think I would have any chance of getting into Yale without applying early, and if I didn't give it a shot, I know I would regret it for the rest of my life. Anyway, this long and troubling train of thought got me to actually start on my Yale application. I filled out one of the two copies I have (they accidentally sent one to Joshua Derezin *and* one to Joshua Berezin) in pen, and wrote down everything that I had a question about or hadn't had the time to do yet. Thankfully it is a short list:

Yale Application Things to Do:

- Page 1-1: Answer question about how I became interested; find out my high school's address; find out the date I entered my high school.
- Page 1-2: Mom and Dad's graduation year and degree; decide whether to include my SAT II writing and my PSAT score.
- Page 2-2: Decide whether I want to request financial aid (probably); decide whether to include the fact that I am Jewish.
- Page 3-2 (this section asks for extracurricular activities, hours participated per week, and number of weeks per year, and also distinctions and awards): Figure out how to show the number of hours per week and weeks per year, since it varies depending on what time of year. For instance, I do football for 25 hours per week for ten weeks a year, 45 hours per week for three weeks a year, and five to ten hours per week for the rest of the year. (I think it would be easiest if I just wrote all of this down rather that averaging it all out); decide if I should include Outward Bound in this section.
- Page 3-3: Write the essays.

The list is not as long or as daunting as I would have expected. I finally read the story that my Spanish teacher assigned for summer reading. It was the most boring piece of literature I have ever read and I couldn't even understand half of the words.

►

Tamara Shirdak
Yale Admissions Officer

I think there's a lot of pressure on students. And sometimes that pressure is "Here's the list of things you need to do." In some ways, we've lost sight of what it is we are originally asking people to do—to enjoy learning and to excel in it because you enjoy it. Take an extracurricular because you want to do it. I feel like the anxiety has forced us to lose some sight in the original purpose of what goes on. It's going to be pretty hard to stop that now.

8/19/96—Despite my exhaustion . . .

Great practice today, despite my exhaustion. Two more days, and I'm done. Didn't do anything on applications.

8/21/96—Yesterday was by far the worst day . . .

Yesterday was by far the worst day I've had this summer. We had a mediocre morning, and the coaches sent us home in the afternoon because we weren't intense enough. They did that twice last year, and I still don't quite understand the logic of it. I mean, if we're down by 14 at the half, what good does it do to quit and go home? I get really frustrated when they do that. I suppose the coaches know what they're doing, though.

So I get home, still pissed off about practice, and suddenly the heavens open and there's this huge storm. Our power went out at about 7:30. My parents and I played a few games of

Scrabble, and then I went to bed. Strangely enough, ours was the only building on the street without power. I felt like I was in a cartoon with a black cloud following me wherever I went.

Today went much better, though. We practiced hard, the coaches were happy, and it was almost as if yesterday hadn't happened at all. Tomorrow is my last two-a-day ever. Let me repeat that: Tomorrow is my last two-a-day ever. I love the sound of that. I can't imagine playing in college and having to tax my body like this for another four years. Next year I'm going to visit some of my friends while they're on college ball teams, sit in the stands while they're practicing, and laugh my head off.

School starts one week from today. Next Monday and Tuesday should be a good time to work on my essays. I know that I'm definitely writing one on football, so I'll try to get that one out of the way.

8/22/96—If she doesn't get in I'll be shocked . . .

Today was a great day to finish off my last preseason. We had a sharp practice in the morning and a motivational speaker in the afternoon. He talked about visualization techniques; he was excellent. I've heard many of these types of talks, but I've never seen one result in such an immediate change in the team's attitude. We all really, truly believe we can beat St. Ed's—and every team after them. We have a scrimmage tomorrow against last year's state runner-up, so it should be a good measure of our progress.

After dinner, I got a call from my buddy Shellie. We talked about our schedules for this year and about how weird it was that we would be seniors, and all that stuff. We also talked about our SAT IIs and APs. (She got an 800 in Chemistry and a 790 in writing, along with fives on a few of the nine APs she's taken—

she pretty much put me to shame.) She's uncomfortable talking about grades and stuff around most people, because she doesn't want to seem conceited, but she knows I'm not going to think that. She's applying to Harvard early, and if she doesn't get in on the first try, she'll apply to Yale and the Ohio State honors program. If she doesn't get into Harvard, I'll be shocked. Shellie deserves it more than anyone else I know.

I know there are two other kids in my school besides her applying to Yale, although I'm not sure if they'll apply early or not. One of them is this dork who always finds it necessary to answer your questions in class, even (especially) when the question is directed at the teacher. By the end of last year, I was ready to beat the hell out of him, but that would have been weak. Plus I would have gotten suspended. Anyway, he has great grades and scores, and he's won a bunch of awards for his poetry, which I think is pretty crappy. The other applicant is a girl with great grades and scores, who just happens to be on the board of directors for the Cleveland Red Cross. Another sort-of-nice person who gets on my nerves. One other kid, Matt, might be applying; he has done really well in school and on tests *and* extracurriculars. He's a cool guy. We sat next to each other in Chemistry, and we always talked about our favorite cartoons from when we were little. I guess the reason why I'm mentioning all of these people is that I realize if I'm going to have this much competition from within my own high school, there's going to be *tons* from around the country. But for some strange reason, I still have that nagging good feeling; I still believe that I can get into Yale.

8/23/96—This is going to be a great year . . .

The scrimmage went pretty well. I fucked up on the first couple of plays, and I'm sure that I won't have a good time watching the films tomorrow. It went well overall, though, so I got home in a pretty good mood. When I got there I found five messages on the machine. I figured the odds were good that one of them was for me, and lo and behold, Elena had called, wanting to know how I was. This is going to be a great year.

Oh, yeah, I got my applications from Michigan and Stanford today.

►

Phil
Middle School Friend

Elena was kind of a lifelong obsession with Josh. Both he and I liked Elena for many years. I love her, and I used to want to go out with her, too, but she's trouble.

8/26/96—This year is going to suck . . .

Saturday night, my parents and I went out with my cousin Sheryll from Chicago. She's very cool. She's a lot older than me (when I was 11 she was 27), so when I was growing up, I never knew exactly how to be around her. Like whether I should call her Cousin Sheryll or Ms. or something. Now she has five kids, and we try to go to Cedar Point with them at least once a year. We went on Sunday and met my younger, very religious cousins from Detroit there. It was fun, despite the fact that ever since I rode on one of those crazy, spinning rides (with Emily, actually), just thinking about roller coasters tends to make me sick. It was good to see all of my relatives, though.

This morning I went to a high school preorientation meeting. Somehow I signed myself up to help out with freshman orientation, so I (and all of the other idiots who got tricked into doing it) had to meet at nine this morning. I guess it was good to see my school friends, but after a while I started feeling like this year is going to suck. I hadn't really thought through the fact that I would have to do homework. I mean, it crossed my mind, but I never fully connected the thoughts with memories of doing calculus at midnight (which hit me at full force upon entering the school building).

After the meeting was over, I went to see my Chemistry teacher, Mr. Rankin, to ask him for a recommendation for my Yale application. He didn't seem all that enthusiastic, although it is sometimes hard to tell with this guy. He has a tendency to examine every aspect of a question and to speak in hypotheticals. Therefore, conversations with him can sometimes be a little disconcerting. Anyway, between the realization that school sucks and the thought of a crappy recommendation, I got pretty nervous. Finally it was time for football practice, so I didn't have time to think about it anymore. Practice was awesome, probably because it was the only one of the day.

►

Mr. Rankin
Chemistry Teacher

I don't write too many recommendations. I would estimate I write five to ten a year. Writing them is not one of my favorite things. It's expected of an advanced placement teacher, so I do it. I don't get paid for it and it costs me time, but it is a duty of the situation because I have good students who are aiming for good things.

I did feel awkward about writing a recommendation for Josh. I knew from the end of the year that I had a very good class of students. There was a nice group of kids who got fives on the AP, but Josh wasn't one of them.

But what went through my mind was: Here was a kid with true grit who worked his heart out for you—who really tried. And when I sat back and thought about that, I remembered seeing someone who bit the bullet and worked hard. And who helped other people with his enthusiasm. I decided, Okay, Josh, I'll give you the benefit of the doubt. I'll go with you.

8/27/96—Tomorrow is just another day . . .

School starts tomorrow. After twelve years of working and waiting, my senior year is finally here. I've been anticipating this moment for a long time, and now here it is. It's a bit anticlimactic so far. When it hits me that I'm actually in my last year of high school, I'll probably feel differently, but at this point, tomorrow is just another day. I didn't even buy new school clothes. Now that I think about it, I haven't bought new clothes in a while. I think that I owned 90 percent of my current wardrobe freshman year. Oh yeah, I helped out with freshman orientation today. It made me remember how scared I was that first day; how I kept on getting lost, and what an all-around dork I was.

Still need to work on my applications. I asked Mr. Pollack for a recommendation, and thankfully he was happy to oblige.

►

Mr. Pollack
Eleventh-Grade History Teacher

Josh was a delight in class. He was very perceptive and I like to think that he has a great crap detector. I give kids numerous readings, never go over them in class but go over a lot of the important ideas, and he was pretty good at siphoning out what's real and what's not real.

8/28/96—It's 10:05, I'm not done with my homework . . .

School sucks. It was nice to see everyone, and all of my teachers seem great, but being there is just a drag. Right now it's 10:05, I'm not done with my homework, and I haven't done anything on any applications. I shouldn't complain (although that doesn't stop me from doing it), because I made this schedule for myself. But somehow I must have forgotten how much homework I had last year. Eighteen more weeks, and I'll be off of *this* hook forever.

It was a little cool to be a senior. I kept looking for my older friends (of course they're gone), and whenever I remembered that our class is on top now, it was kind of a good feeling. I'm really pumped about the game this Saturday. I have this feeling we're going to win. When I get my schedule organized, I will have at least one free period a day, so that should give me a structured period of time to work on my essays. In fact, I'm writing it down in my assignment book, and what I write down in there, I do.

8/29/96—I always thought that was a joke . . .

I'm tired, cranky, whiny (I managed not to bitch about my schedule or my homework load to anybody but my computer), and burned out . . . and it's only the second flipping day of school. Traditionally, the first week of school is not too hard, not too much homework—basically three days to see all of your friends. But if this workload is light, I'm screwed. I got home at 7 P.M., as usual (after a mediocre practice), sat down, started my homework, and it's now 11. There's more I could do . . . if I could stay awake. I worked for about an hour and a half on five Physics problems. I never thought that physics actually involved two trains moving at a certain speed toward each other about to crash; I always thought that was a joke. Of course after spending an hour on that one problem, using every bit of math knowledge I have accumulated since second grade, I still got the answer wrong—by a lot. Hopefully we'll win on Saturday, and things will pick up. I have to stop procrastinating on those applications, but I'm having enough trouble staying afloat without doing them!

8/30/96—No Physics, no girls, no nothing—just football . . .

I can't even begin to describe all the emotions I am feeling right now. Twelve hours away from the biggest game of my life. Three years of hard work and preparation, all for tomorrow. I don't have any idea how I'm going to fall asleep. Everything else that was bothering me is gone. No Physics, no girls, no nothing. Just football. At this time tomorrow, I will either be in the most serene mood of my life or I'll be pretty depressed. I'm betting on serenity.

9/1/96—You never quite know what you did wrong until you see it on film . . .

We lost. We played well but gave up three touchdowns because our punter wasn't kicking well. I hate losing football games. But they were a good team, we needed to play our best to beat them, and it just didn't happen. Life goes on. We still have at least nine more games to get back on track. I also busted my lip and had to get stitches. All in all, it was a pretty crappy day, to say the least. We don't have school tomorrow, but I have to go watch films, which should be an adventure. You never quite know what you did wrong until you see it on film—and then you realize you fucked up big time and cost your team the game. Hopefully I won't have that experience tomorrow (or any time this year). But even if I do, the sun will still come up, and the pain and disappointment will go away as it almost always does eventually. Although I do still think about that one stupid match I lost last year in wrestling.

9/4/96—A weekend to forget . . .

Films were terrible. I looked like crap and got yelled at a lot. It was not fun and not something that I would like to repeat anytime soon. Afterward I went out to eat with a few of the guys, came home, and went to bed. I was exhausted and had a nasty little headache. I guess the fact that I was wearing my left contact lens in my right eye could have contributed to that. I ended up sleeping from three in the afternoon until seven at night, waking up, eating, doing three hours of homework, and going back to bed.

Then Monday rolled around. It was just one of those days. I got up late, which made me late to school, which meant I had to park ten minutes away, which made me late to class, which meant I had to come in early today to make it up, and on and on and on. And yesterday's delight was topped off with a generous helping of shitty practice. All in all, it was a weekend to forget. Today was much better—got to school early, had a good practice. The only problem is that I have tests tomorrow and Friday. They shouldn't be allowed to test you until at least October.

Sunday evening, my dad offered his wonderful insight that the earlier I started my applications, the easier it would be. Gee, Dad, thanks for the advice. Little does he know that I have already looked over Yale's application and made myself a surprisingly short to-do list. The one good thing about having a lawyer for a dad is that when I give him the evidence, he has to concede. Anyway, I figured he's probably right. So at about 11:15 P.M. on Sunday, I sat down and wrote a first draft of an essay for Yale. It's only a start, but at least I have something down. I'm going to forget about it for a few days, reread it over the weekend, and go from there.

9/15/96—A rough week for our hero . . .

It has been a rough week for our hero, Josh. I didn't go out last weekend because I wanted to relax and get caught up with homework, and because I knew the rest of the week was going to be hectic.

Sunday afternoon, after sleeping until 9:00 that morning and doing math homework for about five hours, I got some encouraging news. My dad saw my guidance counselor at the grocery store and she happened to mention the name of Yale's alumni representative in the area, Tamara Shirdak, who just happens to be a good friend of my father. That piece of news motivated me to spend the rest of the day doing homework.

Monday morning, I got an Economics test back and I got an A. Sounds good, but here's where things go down the crapper. Third period all of the seniors met with their counselors as a group. Turns out that the guidance office wants you to have your completed applications in three weeks before they're actually due to the colleges. Bottom line: If I want to meet Yale's early filing date, I will have to get my application in to Mrs. Blattner on the 21st of September, which is kind of soon. So now I'm really nervous and I made an appointment with my counselor for next Monday. From there I went to Physics, where I took a test and basically did not have any idea what the hell was going on. When I got home, I did math homework and wrote out long letters to

Mr. Pollack and Mr. Rankin, formally asking for recommenda-tions. I wrote an extra-long letter to Mr. Rankin, my Chemistry teacher, who seems to be resisting my request, because I want to be sure we're on the same wavelength. Well, I want to make sure he's on my wavelength. So I basically reminded him of what I was like in class, kind of trying to give him words to use to describe me. But I told him in no uncertain terms that if he did not want to write me a recommendation at all, he should please tell me.

I gave both the teachers their letters on Tuesday, along with the recommendation forms from all of the schools except for Penn, whose application is missing in action. Later that day I got my Physics test back. Fifty-three percent. Very nice indeed. Meanwhile, people are starting to ask where everybody is apply-ing. At least five kids are applying to Yale, although I don't know if any besides me are applying early. That night practice went until 7:15 and when I got home I was completely exhausted.

Save for the fact that I had to do 150 Math problems, Wednesday was pretty uneventful. Thursday, on the other hand, was chock full of events. One in particular: a football game. Not just any game, but a *huge* game against a Division 2 state title winner. It was tough concentrating in class all day and I barely made it through. But despite our team's collective excitement and for reasons I don't really feel like explaining, we lost big time. I know I made some big mistakes. I'm not having that much fun with it right now; it's getting really stressful, and tomorrow's films are going to be absolute hell to watch. I wish it could just be fun again. I know that when I look back on it, I will realize how much I loved it, but right now, I'm busting my ass and not getting much out of it. We got back from the game at about 11:30 and I couldn't sleep. Friday, I ended up going to school on about five hours' rest. Even worse than the exhaustion, though, was the nagging feeling that we lost a game that we were capable of winning. I got my Math test back that day and got a 69 percent, which sucks, but it was the best grade in the class. Mr. Schutter said that if you scored above a 60, you're in good shape. There's a new one.

So that was my week. The weekend ended up being just as hectic. It's Rosh Hashanah, and my sister and her boyfriend came in from school. Friday night we had the traditional big meal (one of many over the next couple days)—complete with brisket and kugel and apples with honey—and then went to temple. I don't really like my temple because it's too assimilated—the rabbi gives his sermon through a microphone and they have a choir and an organ backing the cantor up. She has a beautiful voice; I would like it a ton more if they let her do the traditional songs and chants by herself. I know that I am a complete hypocrite, seeing that I hardly ever go to temple, but when I do go, I like to feel Jewish. Besides that, everyone at temple wanted to know where I was going to go to school, so I had to repeat my college speech about 50 times.

Saturday we resumed the big-eating/go-to-temple routine, but in between I managed to find some time to work on my Michigan application. I actually got a lot done, but I have a bunch of questions to ask my guidance counselor on Monday. Saturday night, my family, my sister's boyfriend, and my uncle had dinner (a nice big one) together at our house.

I like my uncle a lot and we have a really good relationship. He is very interested in my college decisions. In fact, he's agreed to help pay for school. Anyway, when he came over he wanted to know if I was applying to Harvard or not. This led to a three-day discussion about why I need to apply to Harvard. The thing is, I didn't really *like* Harvard that much. I had some trouble getting this point across. To him, Harvard is the best school in the country, and I shouldn't deny myself the opportunity to go there if things don't work out at Yale. Meanwhile, everyone is talking like getting into these schools won't be tough, when I actually think my chances are . . . oh, I don't want to guess what my chances are.

Right now I'm kind of bummed. To summarize: I'm not playing well, I'm worried about my grades, I'm worried about going to college, I'm extremely worried about getting into Yale, I need to get my Yale application done in the next two weeks, I need to find a Homecoming date, I'm constantly tired, and I'm already failing. Yup, that about does it.

►

Ken Cohen
Josh's Uncle

I believe that most of the educated public regard Harvard as the best college. I simply felt that Josh should not limit his choices by not applying. Insofar as his not really liking it, I'm convinced that many high school seniors make choices about college influenced, in part, by limited and often irrelevant information. In my opinion, the choice of college should be based principally on the reputation enjoyed by the institution and if there is a particular program in which a student is interested. Many students today, however, choose a college on "how it feels" or on the basis of interviews with two or three students currently in attendance. Otherwise intelligent people who would not dream of generally stereotyping groups will come to the conclusion that all or most of the students at a particular school are "stuck up" on the basis of their experience with two or three students in the course of a one-day visit. I remember one parent friend of mine saying that her son knew he didn't want to attend a particular school the minute he set foot on the campus. What was it? Didn't he like the color of the grass?

9/17/96—Where the hell did the time go . . .

I just spent an hour doing Spanish homework. I was supposed to write an essay about how young people look at the world. The thing is, I just really don't *care* about "how young people look at the world." So I ended up just writing a bunch of nonsense. I know that I need to do well this semester, but I'm just not getting it done. I think it's more an issue of time than of capability (although the more Physics I attempt, the less confident I am in saying that). I met with Mrs. Blattner today, and she wants my application by next Monday. Where the hell did the time go? The only way I could finish all my homework would be to stay up till about 3 A.M., but if I do there's no way I'll be productive tomorrow. I suppose I probably should get used to it now if I plan to go to medical school. And really, I should be working on my application, not sitting here writing.

By the way, the films weren't nearly as bad as I thought they would be—I was even named lineman of the week. I guess my dad's right: I *am* full of shit sometimes. Go figure.

▶

Alec Berezin
Father

Josh is full of shit sometimes. I don't discourage people from being self-critical but he can be overly so. I was always honest with Josh. If he played badly in a football game I told him, and I told him if he played well. I remembered every play—I was really into it. So when he comes back after playing a monster game and says, "Oh, I messed up here and I messed up there," I would say "You're full of shit, you know you played really well." Same thing with saying he failed his AP tests. I told him, "Oh, you're full of shit. You probably got a five." Which he usually did.

9/18/96—Dad jumped at the chance . . .

In terms of news about college, this has been a big week. On Monday I went in to see my guidance counselor, just to clear up my remaining questions about the Michigan application. Surprisingly, she told me that Michigan was pretty close to a sure thing, and not to worry about it too much. That was pretty reassuring, to say the least. That led us into a conversation about my chances at all of the schools I'm applying to. She thinks Yale is a big crapshoot, but no more so for me than for anyone else. She said I had an outside shot at Stanford, a better chance at Columbia and Penn (because of their large applicant pool), but she wouldn't even venture a guess on Brown, thus confirming my suspicions that Brown is funny about whom they accept. All of this was fine. What *wasn't* fine was when she told me she needs everything for Yale but the essay completed by next Tuesday. Ugh. How the hell did I let this sneak up on me? I've had the damn thing for a *month*, and now it's due in a *week*.

I worked on it for about an hour on Monday. I basically just wrote out what I wanted my dad to type on the first of three forms. I also asked my dad to type up my guidance counselor's part of the application. (On every section of the application, regardless of who is to fill it out, I have to fill out a top section with my name, address, social security number, all that stuff.) At my school, the guidance counselors ask that each student give them a summary of everything they've done in high school, and for some reason I have yet to understand, they told the parents they could do this "autobiography" for their kids. Naturally my dad jumped at the chance. So when I gave him the application to type up, he asked if he could do the honors, and I warily said yes. My worries were not unfounded. Before he let me read it, he made it a point to warn me that he got a little carried away. Uh-oh. Actually, most of it was fine, but he added some interesting observations. For example, part of what he wrote was about my religious activities. I have no religious activities. When I go to Detroit and visit my conservative cousins, I'm a religious Jew, but other than that, I am extremely assimilated. He also wrote about how I love to watch nature shows on TV. Granted this may be true, but to read this thing, you would think I had written and produced them. Thankfully, Mom was there to edit his work, and this is what came of their collaboration:

Autobiography

Football—Played four years in high school (two years in junior high), co-captain of football team (12); two-year varsity starter (11, 12), three-year varsity letterman (10, 11, 12); raised money for football team through lift-a-thons, car washes, and other fund-raisers (raised most amount of money during this year's lift-a-thon, more than $600); went with football team to spend a day doing activities with retarded children (see attached letter); summer football training camps (two weeks every summer); off-season training programs (lifting three days per week and running on the other two); many team awards for Camper of the Week, Ironman of the Week, and other such things, a member of numerous "clubs" on the football team (awarded for meeting various criteria like 90 percent attendance in off-season workouts, or meeting certain lifting requirements, talk to Coach Sedmak for specifics).

Wrestling—Wrestled all four years in high school; two-year letterman; off-season training program (offered locally); one week of wrestling camp at Ohio State before freshman year.

Community Service—Almost all community service hours done during the summer. More hours of community service than appear on transcript. Ninth grade: participated in two "service projects" as part of an Outward Bound trip, one involving an overnight stay at a homeless shelter, painting and doing other manual labor; the other involving hauling wood for a man who gave firewood to people who could not afford heat. Tenth grade: Volunteered for about 30 hours over the summer at university hospitals, helping children deal with hospitalization. Also spent five hours volunteering as a parking attendant for a Habitat for Humanity event. Eleventh grade: Participated in Habitat for Humanity's "Building Blitz." Went straight from football camp to East 85 and Quincy, worked four hours a day, and then returned to football for an evening workout. Ended up volunteering about 30 hours.

School Service— (junior year) Went with a group of students with Mr. Pollack to Brush Middle School to discuss issues pertaining to race relations (one day). Participated in freshman orientation (senior year).

Awards—Four-year member of the honor role, received Junior Scholar award from Purdue University for outstanding achievement in the area of Social Studies.

Other Activities

Outward Bound—(Summer 1994) Three weeks in the mountains of North Carolina, hiking, rock-climbing, and canoeing; involved community service

Career exploration—(Summer 1995) Spent a day with a neonatalogist at Rainbow Babies and Children's Hospital, following him as he led rounds through the neonatal intensive care unit. Also spent two or three days shadowing an emergency room physician in a local hospital, observing various medical procedures, included witnessing the death of two patients.

Keeping a journal relating to experiences in college search and admissions process, and other issues relating to being a high school student. Editor suggests this journal may lead to a book project.

Aside from above, Josh will without hesitation go out of his way to do a good deed. He drives several teammates to school on a regular basis, has taken care of both dogs and flowers for friends who are away, without any expectation of payment. I know of these activities only because the parents of his friends thank me, at which point I have to pretend that I know what "it" was that he has done for them or their children. He has amazing self-discipline; he enjoys both physical and mental challenges, as evidenced by the fact that he plays football against much bigger opponents and by his numerous AP courses. He has a fine sense of humor and can relate well to people of a wide variety of backgrounds and ages. He is constantly trying to expand his horizons, both intellectually and socially.

Good, but a little short. Does that mean I haven't done much with my life? In any case, tomorrow I'll turn this in with the info I had my dad type out.

Yesterday I went to talk to Mr. Rankin. He's acting a bit odd, and I'm feeling a bit nervous. He said he'd like to "meet with me" to "discuss the recommendation." He said he would call me at home to set up a time for the meeting. When I asked him if he had my number he said yes, which made me even more nervous. All I want is a simple recommendation. I tried to make it very, very, *very* clear that if he didn't want to write one for me, he needed to tell me very, very, *very* soon.

Meanwhile, Mrs. Blattner came up to me in the library and asked if I got my tenth-grade modern European History teacher,

Mrs. MacDonald, to write me a recommendation, which I
hadn't. Turns out she has a lot of good things to say about me. I
feel bad about not asking her for one. I'll have to talk to her and
explain that the schools wanted an eleventh-grade teacher.
Anyway, I wish Mr. Rankin would write the stupid thing or just
tell me to go elsewhere.

Mrs. Blattner also told me she called the Yale representative
from the area, Tamara Shirdak, and plans to mention my name to
her. They're going to have breakfast together before the conference
on Friday, which I'll be attending (surprise, surprise). Mrs. Blattner
really seems to be pulling for me. She works with about 100 kids,
but it feels like she's going out of her way to get me into Yale. It's
nice to have someone in your corner during this whole thing.

►

Mrs. Blattner
Guidance Counselor

*I think his obsession caught on. I knew how much he wanted to go
to Yale. As much as you try to temper that with realism, it's catching.*

I have to write a letter to my football coach telling him what
I want him to write on his extra recommendation. Stanford is the
only school that gives you a form for a supplementary recommendation, but I think I want him to write me one for Yale, too.
Can't hurt.

Wow. There is too much stuff going on right now. And I
haven't even *thought* about Homecoming yet. Two weeks and
counting. I've gone to it for the past three years, and to tell you
the truth, it's been boring and expensive each time. This year I
want to take someone I'll have a good time with. Otherwise it's
really not worth going. Plus, Homecoming is on a busy day this
year. Obviously I have a game that day, but I also have writing

SAT IIs in the morning. I haven't really prepared for those, either, even though they could be the key to Columbia. Which reminds me, I sent out the release form to ETS—they are sending my official score sheet to admissions offices around the country. Yeehaw.

Oh, I forgot to mention that Mrs. Blattner said the woman who gave the Stanford conference on Thursday night wanted to get in touch with me (I missed it because of a game), so I called her. Apparently, she just wanted to know if I had any questions. I had a few prepared, but after about 30 seconds, I ran out of stuff to say, so I made it up as I went along. My Penn application came today. I feel bad for the kids who are applying early there.

►

Tamara Shirdak
Yale Admissions Officer

We get around 12,000 applicants each year, two-thirds of whom could do the work on campus, but only 17 or 18 percent get in. How do you somehow figure out what students you're going to take to comprise your class? It's tough to pin down what we look for. In a vague way, it is a person who is going to come to Yale, take advantage of what's here, use what's here, even push Yale sometimes, but give back in the process. And students do that in different ways. Some come here and have that perfectly well-rounded look. Some have more of a scientific or academic focus in general as opposed to focusing on extracurriculars. So, our job is to take a student and determine how would they make the most of Yale's campus.

9/19/96—I'm like one of Pavlov's dogs . . .

I got very little sleep last night, so I was really exhausted all day today. Mr. Pollack told me he sent out my recommendations, which is good. Mr. Rankin should follow his lead. I'll kill him if he screws me on these recs.

I was talking to one of the new assistant coaches today before practice started. He went to UVA, and said he always regretted not playing college ball. He offered to call a friend of his on the Harvard admissions committee, to see if there was anything he could do to get me in there, but our conversation was interrupted when the whistle blew. I'm like one of Pavlov's dogs. Every time I hear a whistle blow, I start to run. Practice sucked. We weren't focused and got yelled at a lot. But at least I gave my coach the letter telling him what I need in my letter of recommendation:

Coach Sedmak,

Last week I mentioned that I would appreciate a letter of recommendation from you. As you already know, I am applying Early Decision to Yale. They have a "preferred filing date" of October 15. The deadline for Early Decision is November 1. Also, the guidance office requests that I have my application in to them three weeks before it is due. My counselor asked me to have my entire application in to her by this Monday. Since an additional recommendation is not required, I am not exactly sure if it is necessary for you to give the letter to the guidance office or not. I think that if you could get the letter done before the first of the month, then it would be easier to give it to my counselor (Mrs. Blattner); if you cannot finish it by that date, then it probably would be easier simply to send the letter directly to the admissions office. If that is the case, just tell me, and I will provide a stamped and addressed envelope. When I apply to my other schools in January, I will talk to you again about sending out other letters to other schools. For now, my main priority is getting all of my application materials to Yale in time to meet their deadline.

Yale and all of the other colleges I am applying to ask that you only ask for additional recommendations if there is a person who knows you well and can add something to the application. I think that it is appropriate for me to ask you, seeing that you know me better than any other teacher or coach in the high school. I think there are a few things that would be appropriate for you to write about. First, a brief description of the type of program that we have at Shaker. I have written a lot about football on my application, and I think that it is necessary for the admissions committee to know what you ask of your players. Mostly, though, I think that it would be appropriate for you to talk about my dedication, work ethic, leadership, personality, and other "intangibles." My application does not have anything exceptional (as compared with the rest of the applicant pool) academically speaking. What I need is something that can set me apart, and I think that my work ethic is that thing. Last, admissions officers say that there is nothing better than an anecdote in a recommendation. If there are any stories or situations that you or any of the other coaches can think of that exemplify any of my personality traits, then I think that they would be appropriate to include.

I'm sure that you have written these before, so if you have any other ideas, or don't agree with any of my suggestions, feel free to do your own thing. I'm sorry that I have waited so long to ask you for this so, if you are too busy or can't finish it in time, I understand completely. Thank you very much for doing this for me. I really appreciate it.

If you have any questions, I think you know how to reach me.

Josh Berezin

He told me that he had about a 50/50 record with these applications, and I responded that if I got in to half the schools I was applying to, I would be very happy.

9/20/96—On to Plan B . . .

Another big game tomorrow. We play our rivals from a suburb next door. We've never lost a game to them, and I don't want to start. In order for much of our offense to work I have to play really well, so the pressure is on.

Today was the Yale conference. It was not all that informative, seeing as I have already gathered all the information I could get my hands on and know I'm applying there. Tamara Shirdak, who ran the conference, will also be reviewing my application. Mrs. Blattner did have breakfast with her as she said she would, and apparently she sang my praises. Still, she thought I should introduce myself and try to ask a unique and intelligent question. So I tried to think of some that fit the description, but during Tamara's spiel, other people asked the questions I had in mind, one by one. On to Plan B. When she was done I went up to meet her and asked about social life on campus, and whether people took the train into New York or Boston on the weekends. I figured those were pretty safe.

When I left, I asked the guidance counselor who was attending the conference (not mine) for a pass. She needed my name, but as soon as I said "Josh—" she cut in, "Okay, that's B-E-R-E-Z-I-N." Bemused, I said yeah, but how did she know who I was?

She said Mrs. Blattner had been talking about me all morning and I should make sure to go introduce myself to Ms. Shirdak. Since I had already said hello, I just left. But then I got to thinking. My guidance counselor goes out and tells this lady tons of great stuff about me, I have an amazing chance to meet the person who is reviewing my application, and what do I ask? Do I ask about their History department, or some other interesting topic? Of course not—that might actually help me get in. I ask questions on the most trite and mundane topic I could think of— social life. Good one, Josh. Well, hopefully I'm making too big a deal out of this.

It was funny; the Yale rep was talking about how easy it is to fill out forms one and two of the application. Meanwhile, I spent half an hour last night deciding how to write my address. I didn't quite get why they have two lines for your street address, and I wanted to make sure I got everything right. Four years of high school and AP classes, look where it gets me!

Hopefully tomorrow I can forget about all of this crap for about five hours and thoroughly beat the shit out of the team we're playing.

9/22/96—Just one of those things . . .

We won, 29–3. Even with two minutes left and the score as it was, they were talking shit about how great they are. I'll never understand that.

I went out last night, but it was pretty boring. I ended up at some girl's house with about twenty other people. To be quite honest, I would have been just as happy staying in. I need to find a date for Homecoming. I really don't want to go "as friends" this year, but there doesn't seem to be another option. I don't even know why I feel pressured to go. I never have fun and it's always exhausting. And I have to find a date for Prom, too. So I have *that* to look forward to.

9/23/96—*The calm before the storm . . .*

This week is going to be very busy, and I don't feel like even *thinking* about it right now. All I want is a good night's sleep. The calm before the storm, if you will.

9/25/96—*Oh, Marcia, don't be ridiculous . . .*

Okay, here's the lowdown. I don't have to have my entire application in by October 15, just forms one and two. (Oh, geez, I just thought of a problem. My History teacher already sent in his rec and I don't think they have my name on file yet. I probably should call to make sure that everything is okay.) I already finished those first two forms, I just need to mail them in. I hope. Yesterday my mom found a copy of the typed forms and read it. Then last night I heard my dad say, "Oh, Marcia, don't be ridiculous." I *knew* they were talking about me. So I knocked on the door to their room and asked them what they were talking about. My dad tried to lie, and said there was a problem at Mom's job. I was not that easily fooled, though, and persisted until my mom caved in. Turns out she doesn't like my answer to one of the questions—the only question on either of the forms, in fact, that required any thought at all. It reads "How did you become interested in applying to Yale? Please be as specific as possible (e.g., an aspect of the campus visit, contact with a current undergraduate, etc.)." I answered:

I became interested in Yale after visiting this summer. The admissions representative, Josh Auerbach, was asked to describe a "typical" Yalie, and the person he described was me. After further investigation, I was convinced that Yale is where I belong.

I thought that she was being silly, and said, "Oh, Marcia, don't be ridiculous." After all, I answered the question honestly, and I even used the name of the admissions representative.

This disagreement spurred a discussion about how involved I want my parents to be in this whole process. I told them I felt it would be easier if they kept their involvement to a minimum. My mom wondered whether I was going to have anyone proofread my essays. Of *course* I am, but it is very likely that person won't be one of my parents. I know they're just trying to help, but I feel like I need to know this application is completely mine and no one else's. Sure, I'll ask for their advice, but I wanted it to be clear that I have the final say on everything. I think now they understand how much I appreciate all of their help and how little I want of it.

Maybe that's a bit harsh. I am very grateful to my parents. If it weren't for them and all of their support, I would be a total fuck-up by now. I can talk to them about anything and be sure they'll guide me in the right direction. What I told them, and what I feel, is that it would be easier for everyone if I finish my application myself, show it to them, and have them give me their general impressions.

In any case, I didn't think that my mom had a point in her critique, at first. But then I started thinking about it, and the answer seemed less and less effective. Suddenly I was imagining a letter from Yale saying they would have accepted me but for the horrible answer to that question on Form One. This is a perfect example of why I want to limit how much input my parents give me. I'll end up worrying about the stupidest, most unimportant things. I'm actually almost done, with the exception of the essays.

I have blocked out an hour of time tomorrow just to work on them. I also *need* to talk to Mr. Rankin to see what is going on with that rec.

9/26/96—All in all, it was a bad day . . .

Today was up and down—or rather, first down, then up. I got a few Economics assignments back and found I did pretty poorly on them (29/40 and 16/22). Now my Economics grade is falling. I also had an essay quiz in Economics—it only counted for 15 points of our final quiz average, but it didn't go as well as I had hoped. In the same class—yes, there's more—I have a test tomorrow. And that's only first period. Second period also sucked. We had (you guessed it) a test. Another downer. Then comes the big up of the day, and probably the week: an A on my Physics test. I would be *really* ecstatic about it, except with my last grade, my average is still a D. Finally school ended, but then there was football practice, which, unfortunately, like every other practice this year, didn't go so well. All and all, it was a bad day. If I had done poorly on my Physics test, it would have been terrible. At least tomorrow is Friday.

Still no date for Homecoming. Yesterday in homeroom, they passed out a "Senior Superlatives" sheet. It has subjects like "best dressed," "best smile," "most likely to become President of the United States," and so on. I think I have "most stressed out" pretty much locked up.

9/29/96—College admissions may be indirectly related to one's facial hair . . .

We kicked butt yesterday. The headline in the paper read "Shaker Line Dominates, Beats Lakewood 34–8." They were supposed to be the tenth-best team in the area. Whatever. Yesterday was the first time this year I really had a good time playing football.

Tonight I went to a two-hour Penn conference. It was pretty boring. I went in wearing a shirt with SHAKER written on it so the admissions rep would recognize me. The only problem is that I forgot to shave. It's pretty ridiculous that college admissions may be indirectly related to one's facial hair.

9/30/96—Finally . . . some encouraging news . . .

The time I have to get my Yale application done is rapidly disappearing. Today I got a bunch of tests and stuff back in Economics. I'm really doing well in that class. I think I have something like a 98 percent, if you don't include last week's low grades. I didn't expect to do so well on the test or the essay question, either. It's amazing what can be accomplished with a good teacher, a motivated student, and an interesting topic. I also got an A on my English test. During lunch I went to see Mr. Rankin again about my recommendation. Finally I got some encouraging news from him. He had reread my letter to him last night and had a few questions. (He asked if I was the captain of my football team. Technically, I told him, I am the co-captain. But I asked my coach about it later in the afternoon, and he said I could say captain, because that's what he called me. Coach said he'll show his rec to my guidance counselor tomorrow, just to be sure it's okay.) Mr. Rankin told me he had obtained a copy of my transcript. I told him I felt violated. I thought those were confidential. In any case, he said he would finish my Yale rec within the next 24 hours. I'll pick up his rough draft tomorrow morning so I can look at it, and then we can go back and edit it together. This is exactly what I was hoping to hear.

Tomorrow there is *another* Penn conference. It's being held by the same guy who gave the downtown one last night. I don't know why I'm going twice—I guess I feel like it'll give me more of a chance to make an impression. I'm going to shave this time. Yesterday I asked him a tough question on crime, so he may actually remember me. Good thing, considering he will be reading my application.

I got a lot done on my Yale application tonight. The only thing I still need to know is whether I should include every award I've gotten on the football team, no matter how insignificant. I'll ask Mrs. Blattner tomorrow. Anyway, I went back to the drawing board on my first essay. The topic is "Please write an essay about an activity or interest that has been particularly meaningful to you. We ask that you limit your response to the space provided." I think I've come up with one essay that answers the question pretty well but is not too original. The other one is really creative, but I'm not sure if it answers the question.

Idea Number 1

Last summer I had a conversation with my football coach about applying to college. We were talking about how I would respond to a question like "What makes you special?" if it was asked of me during a college interview. Jokingly, he said that I should point out the fact that, at 5 foot 8 and 200 pounds after a big meal, I am a two-year starter on an offensive line where the other four players average 6 foot 2 and 273 pounds. We both had a good laugh and continued to talk about applying to college. So now, half a year later, here I am trying to write an essay about how football was a meaningful experience to me. After thinking for hours and hours about what football has meant to me, I recalled my conversation with my coach, and realized that football has meant so much to because it has showed me how I could become the smallest kid on the offensive line.

It certainly was not an easy task. The first order of business was to assess my strengths and weaknesses. I knew that if I wanted hang around with the big boys, I was going to have to be strong. Up until about the eighth grade, I couldn't even do a push-up. I would lie on the floor, sweating profusely, trying to push my body off the ground without using my knees like the girls did. Basically what I am saying is that I am not endowed with a huge amount of natural strength. So when freshman football was over, I went into the weight room and started lifting. I lifted with the team in an organized workout every Monday, Wednesday, and Friday for about an hour after school. From that point on, I attended every workout that I possibly could.

Being in the weight room was not enough, though. My friends, the people whom I would be competing against, were there, too. So I had to lift harder than them and do everything with better form.

The other thing I knew was that I was going to need to work on my speed. On Tuesdays and Thursdays we had running workouts, which I treated the same way as lifting sessions.

I also worked hard during the season. I have never missed a practice in all four years of high school football. I cannot even recall a time when I have been late to a practice. Like the off-season running workouts, simply being there was not enough. I had to do every drill as hard as I could, come off the ball as intensely as I could every play, and run as fast as I could on every sprint. Then I had to come back the next day and drill a little bit harder, come off the ball a little quicker, and run a little bit faster.

After all of my hard work and perseverance, I have now started in 16 straight games, with four more to go. So, the moral of the story is that with hard work and perseverance, anything is possible. Not really. If, during this off season, I worked as hard as I have for the past four years, I would still not have any chance of playing big-time college football.

If I have no prospects for continuing my football career, then why is it meaningful to me? Football showed me the value not only of hard work and perseverance, but of working harder and persevering more than others. For instance, I know that I am nowhere near the most intelligent or talented person in my class. What I am is the hardest worker. I succeed not because ideas and concepts come easily to me but because I go home and struggle with them until they make sense. Sometimes that lightbulb goes off after five minutes, sometimes it goes on after five hours. Either way, I will sit there and work until I understand. That is what being the smallest kid on the offensive line has taught me, and that is why football has been a meaningful activity in my life.

Idea Number 2

I can't believe that it's raining on a Tuesday again. When we have our film session on Monday, it's beautiful. When we have our defensive practice on Wednesday, not a cloud in the sky. Thursdays it's special teams on a glorious fall afternoon. But of course, today, when I have to snap that slippery muddy ball with these slippery muddy hands into the slippery muddy hands of that quarterback, it's a torrential downpour.

"Andy," I say to the quarterback, "I can't feel your hand, could you give me a little more pressure." What the hell am I doing here in this freezing cold rain, asking my buddy to push his hands farther up my butt?

"No problem, Josh," he says to me. He calls the play, "146 Z outside post corner motion on two. Ready . . . break."

Okay, 146 Z outside post corner motion on two. No problem, I just block down for the pulling guard and . . . oh, no, they shifted defenses, got to call my guard down, I can't remember the snap count, I'll try two.

"Set hut . . . hut" Andy barks, so I close my eyes and hope for the best. Everyone else goes on the same count. Phew, I got that right. Now I just need to block this guy and. . . .

"Tweet, tweet, tweet." Uh-oh, a whistle that soon can't possibly be good news. "Center and quarterback, get down and give me ten." We fall to the disgusting ground, ignoring the fact that we have thrown ourselves into a huge puddle. Getting our hands wetter will not help us on the next snap. But to protest would be sentencing ourselves to laps after practice. My coach continues his lecture while we do our push-ups. "Berezin, I was a center when I played, and I snapped in much worse rain than this, and I never, in my entire career, have ever fumbled a snap. Get up and run the damn play."

I get ready to snap the ball again. I feel that I'm not going to be able to get it back. I look to the assistant coach, silently pleading with him to wipe off the ball. No such luck. Well, I can always use that trick I learned last year, I'll just put the ball farther back so it will have less distance to travel. Okay, the play was 146 outside. . . .

"Tweet, tweet, tweet." This time the whistle comes from a coach on the sideline. "Berezin, your head is over the line of scrimmage, that's a five-yard penalty."

My head coach chimes in again, "Berezin, don't try to put the ball farther back just so the ball will have less distance to travel. Could we pllleeeaaseee run this play, it's the last one before sprints."

Okay, so that didn't work out so well. There's always snapping it back slowly. It's the last play, might as well. I go over the play one more time, got the snap count. Andy barks out the signals. Almost in slow motion, I give him the ball through my legs. I hold on to it for dear life. My whole purpose at this moment is to make sure that he gets that ball. This time I'm sure he's got it, I can feel that he's got it. My only problem now is that snapping the ball slowly gives that three-hundred-pound monster across the line of scrimmage a chance to get off the ball quicker, and that means. . . .

Wham! That three-hundred-pounder's helmet has just been formally introduced to my chin. I feel my teeth biting through my lip, the blood dripping down my face. I fall down, a flash of light going off in my head. I get up, stunned, but see that we've gained five yards. Thank God, practice is almost over. Just have to finish those sprints. I pull up my girdle, which has been falling down all during practice. What an affront to my masculinity, I have to wear a girdle.

I run through the mud out of breath, wet, cold, muddy, bloody, and demoralized. What am I doing here? Why don't I just quit? As I'm running sprint number 17, I figure it all out. I'm here because this is who I am. I am a player. An out-of-breath, wet, cold, muddy, bloody, demoralized player.

I think I'll ask Mrs. Blattner her opinion of my two ideas tomorrow. Right now it's 10:45, and I still need to shave, so I'll stop writing.

10/1/96—I wish I could just turn my brain off for a few hours . . .

Today was a good day for our hero. Mrs. Blattner read my essays and she liked them both, although she didn't think that the first paragraph of the first essay was any good. She suggested I work on the first essay for Yale and save the other one for a different application. She agreed that the second piece was clearly more interesting, but tying it into the question would be too time-consuming, especially since I only have a matter of *days* to finish that application. That conversation was helpful. She said my rec from Coach was wonderful and thought it could make a difference. Plus she told me the comments from Mrs. MacDonald, my sophomore year History teacher, were particularly excellent. (At the end of each year, every teacher is asked to turn in a sheet for each student that says what that person was like in class.) I really wanted to get a recommendation from Mrs. MacDonald, but I needed one from a junior year teacher, and Mr. Pollack, who also teaches History, is already writing me one. Mrs. Blattner is going to ask her to write an additional letter in my favor for Yale, which can be attached to my application. Mrs. Blattner also said she would include the fact that she had asked me to quit football over the summer in her comments as a demonstration of my dedication. So my meeting with Mrs. Blattner was productive. Later on I went to see Mr. Rankin about *his* recommendation. He had finished it and let me read it. It wasn't good exactly, but it wasn't really bad. I'm showing it to Mrs. Blattner tomorrow, so I'll see what she has to say.

►

Mrs. Blattner
Guidance Counselor

I feel Josh has as much a shot at Yale as anybody, mostly because of his drive and determination and the way he is looked upon by the faculty at our high school. All the teachers are crazy about him because of his discipline and enthusiasm. He's not going to whine and ask "Why do we have to do this?" He's going to sit down and do it. I was talking recently to a teacher who was going to write Josh a recommenda-

tion, and someone else interrupted, "Do you need another recommendation for that kid? I would love to write one for him." That's the kind of feeling that people have for Josh. I'm not sure that he's necessarily the best candidate for Yale as far as numbers and grade point average, but I think the references can make the difference.

All in all, my day was pretty good, until tenth period when I *freaked out.* (A fairly frequent occurrence for me. Generally, I start rambling and hitting my head against the wall, occasionally emitting grunts of frustration. I don't know how else to describe it, but if you saw me, you'd definitely think, "Geez, that guy's freaking out.") My panic started as I was talking to a friend who had just got back from visiting Yale and is thinking about applying early there. Actually, what upset me was his lament about not having a Homecoming date, which reminded me that I didn't have one, either. Thinking about Homecoming led me to thinking about football, then about the one week I have to finish my Yale application. Sometimes I wish I could just turn my brain off.

My dad just got off the phone with Dave Schachter, an old friend who is now a West Coast alumnus interviewer for Yale. We had breakfast with Dave's parents, who still live in Cleveland, over the weekend, and they suggested I talk to him and pick his brain. My dad told Dave he could call tonight, so I guess any prospect of a good night's sleep is once again out the window.

10/6/96—"High School Youths Arrested in Brawl"

So I talked to Dave in California, but the only thing he could do for me was wish me lots of luck. I worked on my essay, too, and just finished revising it tonight. I have a meeting with Mrs. Blattner tomorrow to discuss it. I just let my parents read it, and they thought it was good. We'll see what Mrs. Blattner says. Anyway, I've had a lot of homework and have been in a pretty crabby mood because of it. On Thursday I went down to the gym area to get ready for football practice. Coach Sedmak asked me if I had seen the article in our local paper, the *Sun Press*. I didn't know what he was talking about so he explained. A couple of weeks ago, after our game with our cross-suburb rivals, a few of the guys from their team came over to our school to start a fight. They ended up getting in a brawl with some Shaker kids, but none of our players was involved. The local newspaper came out this week featuring a piece on the fight, complete with quotes from our principal implying that Shaker players were involved. (Our principal says that he was misquoted; he actually said Cleveland Heights players were involved.) Coach was really pissed off. He was mad at the paper and at our principal. When I got home from practice that night, I wrote a letter to the editor and had everybody sign it before yesterday's game.

To the Editor,

The Shaker Heights High School football team would like to respond to the October 3rd article entitled "High School Youths Arrested in Brawl." We feel as if some of the facts have been misconstrued. The article quotes our principal, Dr. Rumbaugh, as saying that "some of those involved were on the football team" and that it is "embarrassing to us as a school." The article goes on to further quote Dr. Rumbaugh as saying that "Athletics is just an excuse for this kind of stuff. We're going to work through the coaches to try to solve these problems. . . ."

First of all, the football team wishes to make it perfectly clear that NO members of the team were involved in the fighting. Every football player was either at a pre-practice meeting or at a conference with a teacher for extra help after school. We feel as if the statements of our principal insinuate that we were directly involved in the incident. Again, this is a complete falsehood. Whether or not Dr. Rumbaugh was quoted correctly is another issue, but either way, the *Sun Press* should have checked their facts before going to press.

We find this article distressing for a number of reasons. Primarily, the article gives the community the wrong impression about our program. Up until a few years ago, the football team enjoyed very little success on the field. For a number of years, we were consistently among the area's worst, putting in 0–10 and 1–9 seasons. Over the past four years, though, the team has posted 6–4, 10–1, and 6–4 records, with a current record of 4–2 (and number 19 in the current *Sun Press* poll). The coaches and players have worked tremendously hard to turn this program around, and we are now a very well-respected program within our community. Our coaches have taught us that being a good football player is secondary to being a good person. We turned the program around not because we are amazing football players but because we are dedicated, hardworking, and disciplined. This article does not portray us as the classy players and people we are. Rather, it depicts us as a bunch of thugs. By not checking your facts, the *Sun Press* has taken away the respect that we have worked so hard to earn.

Besides taking away our respect, the *Sun Press* has also missed a chance to highlight a team that has been an active contributor to its community. As individuals, members of the team take an active role in extracurricular and cocurricular activities. For instance, many members of the team are MAC (Minority Achievement Committee) Scholars. These people act as role models to African-American underclassmen, giving them someone to look up to and emulate. Many other members of the team participate in youth groups and other types of community service. The football team is setting the example for the rest of the school, not vice versa, as the article seems to imply.

As a final note, this past summer, the football team went on a one-day trip to the Metzenbaum Center in Geauga County. We spent the day helping mentally retarded and developmentally disabled children enjoy things that we take for granted. There were no incentives for going and no punishments for staying at home, yet we filled a school bus with players who were willing to give up some of their free time to help someone in need. Enclosed is a copy of a letter that the director of the Metzenbaum Center sent to our coach. We think that it will speak for itself and that it will show what kind of people are on the Shaker Football team. Maybe the *Sun Press* should have written an article about that, instead of falsely accusing us of being an embarrassment to our school and to our community as a whole.

> *Respectfully Yours,*
> *The Shaker Heights High School Football Team*

Everyone signed it, and my dad is hand-delivering it to the editor tomorrow morning. That night we won our game 32–12. We beat the crap out of a pretty crappy team. It was the most boring game I have ever played in.

On the bright side, there's a lot going on this week. First of all, we play the team that beat us for our league crown last year. I know that it sounds very stupid and juvenile, but it was—and is—a big deal. Lots of things in football are like that. Sometimes even I have to laugh when I'm getting screamed at for stepping with the wrong foot. I mean, honestly, is that, in and of itself, going to change my life, or even my game? On the other hand, I have put tons of time into the sport, and I take it very seriously.

The morning of the day of the game I have to take my SAT II writing test, which I am still unprepared for. Plus I have a paper due on *Beowulf* for Monday, but that shouldn't be bad. So besides the football game, I suppose there are only two things that will cause any major anxiety. First and foremost, I need to finish my Yale application this week. I'm really almost done, but the deadline idea (among other things) is making me very nervous. Then I have to wait at least two months to know whether I've been accepted, and if Yale doesn't want me, it may be another six months or so before I find out how the whole thing is going to turn out. Second, Homecoming is this Saturday, the same Saturday as the tests and the game. It doesn't look like I'm going. Not that I couldn't have gotten a date. I know of at least five girls who would have gone with me if I had asked them. It wasn't even that I was afraid they would say no. It was more that if they didn't want to go with me enough to ask me, then we wouldn't have a good time together. Come to think of it, that's part of it, but probably not the real reason, if we are going to be totally honest here. It was more the fact that I didn't think that anybody really wanted to go with me in the first place. Once in a while, I have self-confidence lapses where I don't have very much at all. I usually can muster up enough gumption to ask a girl to Homecoming, but I just didn't do it this year. People have asked me who I'm going with, and when I tell them

I'm not going, they say "Awww." I tell them that I didn't really want to go anyway. I almost believed it myself for a while, but now that it's here, I do want to go, but it's too late. Actually, it's not. There are still some people I could go with, but none I would have asked in the first place. I don't know, the whole thing sort of sucks, and I can't decide if I am really upset about it or not. It's a little confusing. It must be the hormones. My point is that everything seems to be coming apart at the seams this week, just when I need to hold it together. And just when I wouldn't mind it being a little bit nice—or at least normal.

10/8/96—It's all coming down . . .

Tests, papers, Homecoming, football, college. It's all coming down this week. Was up until 1:30 doing essay last night, going to get a good night's sleep and turn this week around.

10/10/96—I can see myself in maize and blue . . .

Well, this hellish week is almost over. I had—and have—a lot of stuff to think about, and I haven't really sorted it all out. First, there was Yale. Except for tonight, I didn't work at all on my application (not to mention all the others piling up), yet I spent the majority of the week thinking about it. On Wednesday I went to two college conferences: Michigan and Columbia. The Michigan conference made me realize that I probably wouldn't really mind going to Michigan—if I don't get into Yale, I'll have to visit Michigan again to reassess. I'm almost positive that I can get in there, and I can see myself in maize and blue. The guy from Columbia was really funny. He was very easy to talk to and excited about the school. I think Columbia is my second choice at this point. I hope I get in somewhere.

I also had to think about high school this week—for a change. Unfortunately, I didn't do too good of a job. I studied, but not very well. Thankfully I didn't have too many tests this week, although I'm now behind in my homework.

Tomorrow I have to cram like hell for the SAT II tomorrow. It's hard for me because the test consists of all these instances where you have to correct other people's mistakes. My grammar is not terrible, so when I write I can put together sentences that work, but for some reason, I have trouble finding errors in other people's constructions. And then there's the game. We should be able to beat the team we're playing, and I have a feeling we will. This is an important game for us. We need a win to have a chance at being league champs. Right now, though, I'm not all that pumped. I've been excited in practice, and I know I will be intense come game time. Then there's Homecoming. I definitely do not have a date. I'm going to hang out with a friend who doesn't have a date, either. We're skipping the dance and going straight to the parties afterward. This could be the best time I've ever had at Homecoming . . . or the absolute worst.

I've been in a rotten mood all week. I've tried to talk to people about it, but I end up sounding incoherent. Most of it is because of Homecoming, I think. (I did a bad thing today. I told my friend that there were no girls left to take to Homecoming, right in front of a girl who didn't have a date. I realized it right after it came out of my mouth. I've been offending people right and left lately.)

10/13/96—Seven girls came up and hugged me, yet I couldn't find one date . . .

Believe it or not, this weekend turned out pretty good. On Saturday I woke up early to take my writing SAT II. I don't think I did very well. Many of my friends who are in AP English had trouble with the test, too. But I felt better once it was over and was as pumped up for the game as I've ever been for any sporting event. (Probably part of it was the exhilaration of not having that test hanging over my head anymore—I guess it was bothering me more than I thought.) We beat them all up and down the field. We scored twice on defensive touchdowns and our offense looked good. It was incredible. Those dudes thought they were so sweet. I guess they just weren't sweet enough.

If I was pumped before the game, I was *really* pumped after the game. It took me a good five or six hours to really calm down. I had bumped into Alex (he came home from school for Homecoming) at the game and made plans with him for that night, but in the few hours he was home he found a date for the dance. So I met up with my similarly dateless friends and we went out to eat. It was pretty fun, but a little pathetic. Then I went to a party for a few hours. It's funny, once I was there, seven girls came up and hugged me, yet I couldn't find one date for the dance. I wouldn't hug most of them back. I just didn't think they deserved it. I've been doing weird shit like that all week. After the party, I went over to Jessica's house and was out till around 3. A grand finale for a really good day.

I was really moody today, probably partially an aftereffect of last night's festivities. I didn't get enough sleep because I woke up early this morning to work on my essays. I finished most of them and just need to give them to an English teacher to proofread. But I kept thinking about applying to Yale. I'm not having second thoughts about Yale itself, I'm just wondering if I'm doing the right thing, using the right strategy. I mean, let's say I don't get into Yale, *and* I don't get into any of the other schools I've applied to except for Michigan. I'd probably be perfectly happy there, but at the same time, I could have gotten in there without killing myself in high school. Well, too late now—I'm up to my neck.

I gave my essays to my parents to look over. I think my dad thought that I wanted him to rewrite them for me; he made so many suggestions, I got a little mad. Maybe I'm just grouchy. I never thought I'd say this but I'm ready for a good week of school.

10/14/96—"Convincing" is probably not the right word—"annoying" is more accurate . . .

Yale Admissions Office, here I come. Tonight I finished both essays. I showed them to my English teacher from last year, and she loved them. Hopefully I'll get the same response from whoever reads them in New Haven. All I have to do is give them to my dad to type and to find some way to get my essays onto the proper forms. (I know I am supposed to do that myself, but it would take me about a week to feel comfortable using a typewriter instead of a word processor, and besides, he volunteered.)

►

Alec Berezin
Father

Typing Josh's applications was a nice way of finding out what was going on, which I usually do by hocking him a lot. It got to the point where it was too much and we were both getting aggravated. So we set aside a designated time when I could ask him questions. I knew he was under a lot of pressure. He was playing football and taking this ridiculous number of AP courses, which was very demanding. I said I'd do whatever he needed in order to make it easier.

Essay Number One

"Huddle," I yell at the top of my lungs. The quarterback responds to my summons. He stands there waiting for the coach to yell in the next play. Suddenly I lose sight of him, my view obscured by four of the largest human beings I have ever encountered. The quarterback calls the play, but I am unable to hear him through the vast layers of muscle and fat that separate us. I hear my coaches chuckling in the background. Even I have to laugh sometimes. Here I am, at 5 foot 8 and 200 pounds, surrounded by my fellow offensive lineman, who average 6 foot 2 and 273 pounds. It must be a sight to see. Me in the back of the huddle, clawing my way back within earshot of the quarterback, or stretching up on the tips of my toes, straining to read his lips. I finally get the play, hustle up to the line of scrimmage, and run the play. Let's be perfectly honest here. I have no business starting on the offensive line at my high school. There are kids on the team who are bigger, stronger, and faster than me. But here I am, hidden in the back of the huddle, trying to get the play. Football has meant a great deal to me over the past four years. It has given me discipline, confidence, and has taught me how to set goals for myself. More than anything else, though, football has been significant to me because it has shown me what it takes to become the smallest player on the offensive line.

So, how did I become that center in the back of the huddle? It certainly was not an easy task. The first order of business was assessing my strengths and weaknesses. I knew that if I wanted to hang around with the big boys, I would need to work on my strength. Up until about the eighth grade, I couldn't even do a push-up. I would lie on the floor, sweating profusely, attempting to push my body off the ground without using my knees like the girls did. Basically what I am saying is that I am not endowed with a huge amount of natural strength. So when freshman football ended, I went into the weight room and started lifting. I lifted with the team in organized workouts held every Monday, Wednesday, and Friday for about an hour every day, every week of the month, every month of the year. From that point on, I attended each workout that I possibly could. Simply being in the weight room was not enough, though. My friends, the people with whom I would be competing, were there, too. I had to lift harder and perform the lifts with better form than they did. Needless to say, I can now do a push-up without using my knees.

Besides working on strength, I also realized that I needed to work on my quickness. The standard for speed in high school football is the 40-yard dash. Freshman year, I ran the forty in 5.8 seconds, about the equivalent of a speedy garden slug. So on the days when I wasn't lifting, I attended running workouts. Now I run the forty in 5.2 seconds. Still not exactly Carl Lewis, but relatively speaking, a fairly substantial difference.

All of those running and lifting workouts were to prepare me for the regular season. I could have made myself the strongest, fastest kid on the team during the off season, but it wouldn't have done me any good if I hadn't shown up for the real thing. I have never missed a practice in all four years of high school. I have never even been late. Like the off-season workouts, mere attendance was not enough. I had to execute every drill as hard as I could, come off the ball as intensely as I could on every play, and run as fast as I could on every sprint. Then I had to return the next day and drill a little bit harder, come off the ball a little bit quicker, and run a little bit faster.

After all of my hard work and perseverance, I have now started in 17 straight games, with three more to go. So, the moral of the story is that with hard work and perseverance, anything is possible. Not really. If, during this upcoming off season, I worked as hard as I have for the past four years, I would still not have any chance of playing football at Yale or at any other Ivy League school.

If I have no prospects for continuing my football career, then why is football meaningful to me? Football has demonstrated to me not only the value of hard work and perseverance but of working harder and persevering more than others. For instance, I know that I am not the best student in my class, just as I am not the biggest football player on the line. What I am is the hardest worker in the classroom, just as I am the hardest worker on the field. I succeed not because ideas and concepts always come easily to me but because I go home and struggle with them until they make sense. I treat schoolwork the same way I treat practices and off-season workouts; simply doing my work is not enough. I have to work harder and longer than others. Sometimes the lightbulb flashes after five minutes, sometimes after five hours. Either way, I will sit there until I understand. That is what being the little kid on the huge offensive line has taught me, and that is why football has been a meaningful activity in my life.

Essay Number Two

My father can be quite convincing. Actually, "convincing" is probably not the right word. "Annoying" is much more accurate. My dad will bother me and harass me until he gets what he wants. For instance, last winter, the weekend before final exams, my father suddenly became convinced that I could play football in college at the Ivy League level. I had to spend about five hours on the Internet, looking for college rosters, just so I could get him out of my room. Of course, when I finally found the rosters, the players were at least half a foot taller than me and a good 50 pounds heavier. I was right, and he was wrong. I have found, over the past 17 years, that this is the case 99.9 percent of the time. This summer though, my dad came up with an idea that even I admit was one of the best he has ever had.

It all started the day I returned from my visit to Yale this summer. I had completely fallen in love with the college, and I wanted to tell my guidance counselor that Yale was my first choice. Before I entered the office, I thought that she would be enthusiastic about my decision. The meeting went well for a good minute and a half. She was excited that I liked Yale so much, but she did not want me to get my hopes up for admission. She wanted to know what my plans were for the summer, hinting at the fact that a unique summer experience could be the key to getting in. I reminded her that I was working out for the football team every day and that I would be wrestling for at least three days out of the week. This meant that I couldn't exactly have a steady job. As I talked, I noticed that her face began to sag. I was unfazed at the time and continued talking. Since I couldn't be employed, I explained to her, I thought I would try to do some volunteer work. My guidance counselor's face was now in a full-fledged frown, and she even started shaking her head. No, this would definitely not do. I needed a hook, something that was unique and special, not just simple volunteering. I needed to get involved with Junior Council on World Affairs or the debate club. Now my face joined hers in a frown. I explained to her that during the school year, football starts right after school and I'm lucky if I return home by seven. As much as I would like to, I told her, I didn't have the time nor the energy to join an academic club. I thought that would be the end of that and we could move on to her next suggestion. But she started to inform me how I was putting football over admission to the school. She said it would be a different story if I was going to play there, but I told her that I just wasn't big enough. She pushed the issue further and suggested that maybe I should quit football. I was speechless that someone who knows me well would even think about that. After I recovered from my initial shock, I told her that if I was going to quit football, I might as well drop out of school. She said that she understood, and with that in mind, we should try to find something constructive to do over the summer. She asked me if my parents knew any doctors that I could do some research with, and I told her that my dad, a plaintiff's malpractice attorney, had sued so many doctors that it might be tough to find someone willing to help. She said that I would have to find a project, or else my chances for admission would be next to impossible.

I went home dejected and depressed, but not defeated. The two things I love doing more than anything else are over-achieving and proving somebody wrong. So I made some phone calls, and I thought that maybe I had found some people who could help me. Each of the people I contacted called back and told me how late it was to be doing this and that I had little chance of obtaining a position that people had applied for in February. One person responded very enthusi-astically—unfortunately, she told me to look for a volunteer position in the hospital where I had worked last year.

With my connections practically exhausted, I had to turn to my parents as a last resort. My dad suggested that I call a friend of the family in New York. This friend is a little bit crazy, and my dad thought he might be able to come up with something unique for me to do. I felt that this idea would work out about as well as his idea about my college football career. As I've said though, when my dad thinks he has a good idea, he is relentless in seeing it carried out. After days and days of constant pestering, I finally caved in and e-mailed this guy. He responded with a list of thirteen things to do over the sum-mer. Some were funny (go to India without any money, find my way home, and write about my experiences in my college essay), while others were realistic, but not anything that I hadn't previously considered. I figured that I had succeeded in once again showing my dad that he had been foolish. A day later I received a phone call from an editor who told me that she thought I should keep a journal about the college application process and the pressures that a high school senior faces. She thought it would make a great essay topic and maybe even be turned into a short book. I started writing the second I hung up the phone, and haven't stopped since. When I told my mom the good news, she found the whole thing absolutely hilarious. My father also seemed to find humor in it, but I'm still not sure if he was happy about the fact that I may be a published author, or if he was just basking in the glory of having one of his ideas actually work. I'm not quite sure how to feel about this whole thing. There are a lot of different aspects to what this means. First of all, it means that I am almost done with my first application. There's no confusion about that, that's a good thing. But it also brings up other issues. Whether I'm making the right choice is one issue. Another is how ready I am to go to college. I don't feel like staying in high school for another day, let alone another half of a year. I don't know. The whole thing is weird, and I need some time to myself to sort everything out. Unfortunately, I don't have very much time at all. Right now it's 11 P.M., and I haven't even really started my homework. Another late night.

Tomorrow I'm meeting with the guidance counselor in charge of helping kids get scholarships. Hopefully we can find a way to ease the financial burden on my soon-to-be-impoverished parents.

Sound familiar? This plan turned out even better than I thought. Not only am I writing *about* my journal, but I am actually using writing *from* my journal in my application. Pretty cool.

10/15/96—Use the space provided . . .

I don't know if it was yesterday's sprints or what, but I felt like crap this whole day. In fact, I would be in much better shape right now if I had never gotten out of bed this morning. I met with the guidance counselor about financial aid. I got a few ideas, but more important, I found something to do this summer. I think I'm going to participate in this program for high school kids where you go work at a national park for five weeks, restoring trails and building bridges. It is right up my alley.

My dad is having some trouble getting my essays typed up. Actually he is not really typing them at all. The problem is this: If I had just typed the essays, they would have been too long, so I did them on my computer. But the directions specifically tell you to use the space provided. The essays fit, but they wouldn't if I used a normal typeface. So my dad went all over Cleveland today to try to find someone who could do it. You'd think that this would be a fairly easy request, but you'd be wrong. The only person who knew how to do it was some eccentric computer geek who works alone in a loft. He should have them done by tomorrow. I want this whole thing over with! Once this application is in I can relax a bit, although I still haven't finished the Michigan application I planned to do even before starting Yale's. Oops.

I picked my senior quote for the yearbook: "I am glad I did it, partly because it was well worth it, and chiefly because I shall never have to do it again." —Mark Twain

10/16/96—Go, Josh!

Bob Dole is just not with it. I wish I could get more excited about Clinton, but he's such a corrupt bastard that it's hard to get all gung-ho. Tonight's debates sparked a debate in my house about affirmative action. Mostly I think it's a good thing that needs to be preserved. When I talk to my black friends on the football team, it's clear they haven't had the same opportunities that I have. They can sign up for the same classes, but, like one of my friends told me, "I just wouldn't feel comfortable in a classroom full of white kids," and I can't say I blame him. My dad was telling me stories about how some medical schools don't allow teachers to flunk minority students because of affirmative action, and some of these students who should have flunked out are now practicing medicine. Who knows? It's really a big problem. The only issue I have with these programs is that they are just a Band-Aid over larger and more serious problems with society.

No more essays hanging over my head, as long as that freaky printer gets them on there right. Finally! Football's almost over, I can't believe it. And I got As on my last two Physics tests. Go, Josh!

10/17/96—No one seems to believe that I'm too small . . .

I turned the finished application in today and just need to give the school permission to release my transcripts. My dad went through hell to get the essays printed up. That computer guy turned out to be as strange as he seemed. When my father first brought the essays to him, he started to explain that one essay belonged to one question and the other essay belonged to the other one. After about half a second, the guy cut him off, saying he could *tell* that the football one went with the first question and the one about "my annoying dad" went with the second one, and then proceeded to reconfigure his computer programs for my application. It turned out really nice.

So I'm done. All day I was excited about not having to work on my application anymore, but once I got home, I started to worry. My sister's friend's mother called to talk with me. Her son, who went to my high school, got into Yale last year, and she suggested I contact him. Then she asked who else was applying, and I told her about my friend who is an exceptional swimmer. My sister's friend's mom's son (that would be my sister's friend's brother) is also a great swimmer and is now swimming at Yale. Thanks. Then she told me that she thought I could play ball at Yale because their team sucked so much. No one seems to believe that I'm too small. Then she proceeded to tell me about the day he got accepted. It was very nice of her to call, but she brought up every issue I am worried about right now. First, I'm beginning to think that maybe I'm *big* enough to play at Yale, just not *good* enough.

►

Coach Sedmak
Football Coach

Josh was a very good football player. He was somewhat undersized but not what you would call small, really. He was adequate. He did play next to some of the biggest players we've ever had. But his intensity, toughness, and intelligence made up for it. He really was the leader of that offensive line. There are colleges he would have been big enough to play for, but not Yale.

My second concern is that I'm pretty sure that my friend will get in because he is being recruited. (By the way, my sister's friend's mom heard I was applying to Yale through the mother of the quarterback on my team, Andy. He is one of the finest people I have ever met. I know he's received letters from Yale. I hope he's not avoiding Yale just because he knows I want to go there. That's the kind of thing he would do.) My point is I'm starting to get worried. I guess it's both good and bad that I finished the application. On one hand, I don't have to worry about finishing it; on the other, there is absolutely nothing left that I can do to improve my chances of getting in at this point.

We have our second-to-last home football game this weekend. We have an off chance of making the playoffs this year. I can't wait to play in Saturday's game. That team beat us by a small margin last year, and now it's time for some payback.

I didn't do one second of homework tonight and I don't regret it for a minute.

10/23/96—This lazy thing . . .

Wow, have I been lazy in this journal. I'll have to come back and fill in some of the gaps (beating Shaw, stayed at home, coaches being assholes, wrestling, Jason Ward, grades, homework, apathy, Michigan application, worried about Yale). But right now I'll talk about right now. Specifically, this girl in my Spanish class, Elena. We've been friends for a while, and I've always had sort of a crush on her. The thing is, she is flirtatious with all guys, and extremely flirtatious with me. I don't think anyone can begin to imagine what this girl does to me during Spanish class. Without getting too graphic, let's just say she is not shy around me. To give you an idea, let's just say that she likes lollipops and I now know she has a really big tongue (and I mean *really big*. She shows that to everyone, though). But since she's always like that, I have no way to tell whether she is really interested or not. If any other girl treated me like she does, I would be on her in a second. But I just can't tell with Elena. She *has* been calling me a lot recently, and she invited herself over to dinner on Friday. I told her she could come, but it would have to be an early evening because I have to go out with the football team this Friday night. She said okay. Then I asked her if she was planning on going out with me and the guys after dinner, and she said yeah. So I'll see how it goes.

►

Elena
The Girl from Spanish Class

I got to know Josh in Spanish class my senior year. We had freshman English class together but I didn't really know him then. He seemed very smart, like he knew everything. I got to know him better in Spanish class and we got to be really good friends.

We always sat next to each other and talked about weird stuff in class. I liked to tease him a lot. I guess I'm a friendly person, but it was definitely more with him. One day we just started talking on the phone. I think I kind of had the control in our relationship because—he told me this afterward—at the end of junior year and then beginning in the senior year, he had a crush on me. But we were best friends. The more I got to know him, the more I liked him.

Today's practice was kind of bullshit. The offensive-line coach got real mad at us for not being focused. It's gotten to the point that I just tune them out if they start yelling. But still, even with all the crap, I'm going to miss it.

I tried to talk with my Math teacher about quarter grades today. I wanted to make sure I was getting an A, because all my schools are going to see these grades. On the first test of the year, I got a 69. He told me that was good, because eventually it would become an A. So I just want to say to him "Look, I'm doing well and I'm progressing the way you said I'd need to to get an A. I just want to make sure that's being reflected because this semester's grades are really important for me." But he wasn't there, that bastard.

Part Three

▶

Waiting

10/25/96—When a coach threatens me with death, I think it's pretty personal . . .

Today was the last day of the first grading period, and tomorrow is my last home football game ever. We won our last game 35–0, but the coaches thought we should have done better. When we ran during practice this week, the coaches got mad at us for talking during sprints. I wasn't really bothered that they were yelling at us for not being focused (we probably weren't), but what did irk me were their attitudes. Our coaches start yelling at us, seemingly out of the blue, about how we're overconfident, and how we might lose our next game, and all sorts of crap. Now, I usually understand where the coaches are coming from, but not about this. Here we are, with two weeks left in the season, and we aren't allowed to have any fun? Even when we're working hard, we get yelled at. I realize that it's the coaches' job to make sure we play well, but there must be a better way to do that than calling us a bunch of pussies. It's tough to get hollered at week after week after week—especially by people you respect. I'm getting really sick of it.

The next day our offensive-line coach worked the hell out of us. After the session, I couldn't even walk. Every time I would bend my knees, they would buckle, and I was crawling around the field until my legs stopped feeling like pudding. It was incredibly hard, but it was also one of the best team practices I have ever been a part of. Coach Sedmak even said we did a good job. The coach who was pissed off at us on Monday ran the practice. He's a really great person, even though he was acting like an asshole that day. I think they are trying to keep us focused for next week's game. Tomorrow we're playing a team that is zero for eight—we should kill them.

Coach told us today that we had a bad week, as if I couldn't tell. I don't know, he may be right, but the more they yell, the more I lose my intensity. I don't want to come to practice knowing that we're going to get belittled. I know that you're not supposed to take it personally, but, call me crazy, when a coach threatens me with death, I think it's pretty personal.

Tonight I went out with the team to scout out next week's opponent. We do this every week, or will until the season ends. We saw the team we'll oppose next week play the team we beat two weeks ago. The latter team won, which means that we probably can win tomorrow and will clinch a tie. All I know is tomorrow is the last time I play on our field, and I'm going to enjoy it if it kills me.

Before I went out with the team, Elena came over for dinner. I think I might be starting to fall for her. If we had a normal relationship, I would know that she was interested, too, but like I've said before, somehow we just don't.

10/26/96—I'm not happy being a player, and I wouldn't be happy being a slacker, so where does that leave me?

I had always thought that playing my last home game ever would be really emotional, but it really wasn't—or at least not yet. I may start to cry once I get into bed and really start to think about it. Right now I'm kind of depressed. I'm depressed that I'm not more sad about playing my last home game. Wow, that's screwed up.

We won the game 45–12. (We were leading 38–0 at the half, then they took the starters out.) It was pretty damn boring, especially the part where we got yelled at yet *again* for not being focused. That could be why I'm not more upset about the season ending; I'm just really sick of getting yelled at. Before the game started, we had the traditional ceremony where the seniors are recognized and present flowers to their parents. I think the ceremony was more emotional for my parents than for me, which makes me kind of mad. I'm mad that I'm not more upset, because at least if I'm mad, I'm feeling *something* about this huge piece of my life ending. If I didn't feel anything that would mean I don't care, and if I don't care, I wasted the better part of the past four years of my life. I don't know what else I would have done with myself, though. Even if I didn't play football, I don't think I would be a huge partier. I don't know, but I think that getting wasted would have lost its appeal very quickly. So I'm not that happy being a player, and I wouldn't be happy being a slacker, so where does that leave me?

I still have no girls (surprise!). It's not just the physical stuff I miss. I think it would be nice to have someone to be with. But I don't think anyone I know would be good for me on that level. Whenever I try to imagine a person I'd be with forever, I can't. I can't even fathom what the person who'd want to be with me forever would be like. It's going to be tough to find someone I like and who can put up with my junk. Who knows? I'm all screwy right now because I'm nervous about wrestling season. I don't know what to expect from myself this season, and I don't know where to set my goals. As tough as football has been, I'd still rather play ball for the next five months than wrestle. So why am I doing it again?

10/27/96—Schools are worried only about memorization and regurgitation . . .

I was a lazy bastard today. I hardly did any homework. Actually, I worked for about three hours or so, but I didn't get much of anything done. I just can't seem to get excited about derivatives or cost curves at the moment. In a way, school is kind of stupid. It's not really geared toward learning, which is a bit odd. Schools are worried only about memorization and regurgitation. I guess I shouldn't make such a broad generalization. Some of my teachers are very committed to making sure I have a good grasp of the subject they're teaching. Actually now that I think about it, most of my teachers are good people who are trying to make a difference. I'm probably just looking for an excuse not to do my work, so I'm blaming America's educational system. I think I'll do some Economics before I go to bed. I want to get a lot done this week, and hopefully I'll get back on track.

I'm starting to have second thoughts about some of the decisions I've made in high school. Right now, as evidenced by the incoherent previous paragraph, I'm pretty stressed out and not exactly enjoying a wonderful senior year. If I get into more than one school, it will have been worth it, but as it stands, that's a pretty big if. A lawyer in my dad's office went to the University of Michigan and majored in History but she was leaning toward pre-med, just like me. She wants to talk to me. I didn't want to at first, but I think I definitely should.

Some of the other teams in my school are finishing up their seasons this week, and they're all crying and everything. I haven't cried in about four years. I remember crying about something stupid, and then realizing "Oh, man, this is bullshit. I'm not going to do this anymore." I even want to sometimes, 'cause it can make you feel better, but I just can't. I think I will on Saturday, though. I think the anticipation of that is part of why I'm feeling so weird about everything right now. That and those raging hormones.

10/29/96—I think we've arrived at a mutual understanding . . .

Today I found out one of my friends is applying early to Princeton. Usually I wouldn't care, but he's been a swimmer and has a good chance of getting in wherever. I actually encouraged him to apply to Yale instead. God knows why.

There was a Brown conference at the high school tonight. Before I left for it, my parents and I were talking about my applications. My mom let it slip that she had called my guidance counselor to find out if my Yale application had been mailed. Ordinarily, I wouldn't have been upset, but for the past three nights, my dad has been bugging me about what was going on with my applications. Every time he brought it up, I would tell him *I was taking care of them.* As much as I appreciate my parents being involved in my college decision, I want it to be my accomplishment, not theirs. I'm trying to make this process mine as much as I can. I thought I had made it clear that I didn't want them doing things like that. To me, that's like going over somebody's head at work. I started screaming at my mother, and banished her from any and all involvement with my college stuff. I think she was pretty upset, but I was, too. My dad and I left for the Brown conference soon after, and he cooled me off. He made fun of all the people asking silly questions. One girl asked about Brown's Egyptology program; another wanted to know if she should get letters recommendation from her professors in Europe. Inane questions like these made the conference go on until about 9:30. It was really ridiculous. If I had been paying attention, I would have known more about Brown than people who are already enrolled there. When I got home I apologized to my mom for upsetting her, but I told her I still thought she was wrong for calling behind my back. I think we've arrived at a mutual understanding. From now on, I'm sure she will come to me first, and we can avoid another major war.

►

Marcia Berezin
Mother

Josh got pretty pissed off at me for calling the guidance office. He was a little hypersensitive but he just wanted the whole thing to be from him. I could understand, but on the other hand, he goes to a fairly large high school and, though they're very well organized, mistakes happen and sometimes applications don't get sent out. It would be very sad if that happened. If it hadn't gotten out, then I'd have been a hero for calling. But instead I got into trouble.

10/31/96—Just a stupid test . . .

There were two pieces of mail for me today. The first was my SAT II writing score: 650. Yes, that's right, six hundred and fifty. Ten points *less* than my previous performance. There goes

Columbia. Actually, I'm not all that worried about it. I'm more annoyed that I can't seem to master the English language. Oh, well, just a stupid test. The other item was a postcard from Yale confirming the receipt of forms one and two. So they know my name in New Haven at least—it's a start. It's kind of bizarre that some other people who I've never met are going to be deciding my future. Every time I see my relatives, they ask me where I got accepted. Well, I've only applied to one school so far, and I probably won't get in there. I *must* finish my Michigan application. People have been mean to me all week, blah, blah, blah. (Sometimes I have weeks where it feels like no matter what I do, someone yells at me, mocks me, belittles me, or otherwise makes me feel small. Maybe I'm just paranoid. Maybe I wouldn't be so paranoid if all those people would stop following me.)

11/1/96—Hence the name "senior tackle"...

Last game is tomorrow. Last practice was today. Every year on the last day of practice, we do this thing called "senior tackle," where a sophomore or junior roasts a senior. Aaron *really* roasted me. He talked about how small I am, and how I haven't had a girlfriend in four years of high school. (This is actually not true, I did have one during freshman year, Louise Burton. We went out for about two weeks.) After the junior says his piece, the senior gets to hit him, hence the name "senior tackle." I wonder if I'll feel any different tomorrow. It will probably hit me on Monday when I don't have practice after school. Next August is going to be strange without two-a-days. As tough as football is, I have a feeling I won't be whole without it. I know it sounds corny, but it's true. I'm going to miss everything—the coaches, the players, the sprints, the broken fingers, everything. I don't really want to think about this right now, it's too weird. I'll write more tomorrow when it's all over.

Got my report card today, got a B in English. I could have gotten an A but I fucked up on the last two assignments. What're you gonna do? A 4.8 for the quarter is good enough for me. I've got a lot of work to do this weekend, but I just can't concentrate right now. I'm going to try to get some sleep.

11/4/96—Why are girls so god-damned confusing?

So I cleaned out my football locker today and brought home about four months' worth of dirty, nasty, smelly, moldy clothes.

At least I ended my high school football career on a good note. We won the game, won the league, and ended up 8–2. We didn't make the playoffs, but there's nothing we can do about that. It really wasn't as emotional as I thought it would be. I'm more upset about the team breaking up than about not playing the game anymore. After four months of being on the receiving end of all that screaming and yelling, you get to be pretty close. You end up standing up for one another and supporting each other. Of course, people got annoying sometimes—I know I did—but that's natural.

Now I'm taking a few days off, relaxing, and catching up on all of my non–sports-related stuff. Like TV. Ha. Wrestling practice starts on Friday, though, so I shouldn't get too used to the early afternoons. Aaron came over for a while on Saturday after the game and I ended up having a pretty good time despite my bad mood. We just hung around—watched TV and talked to my dad. Elena called before he got here. I don't know what the hell's going on with that chick. She keeps on calling and being really nice to me, but now I hear she's got a new boyfriend. Why are girls so god-damned confusing? So anyway, on Saturday night Aaron and I drove around Shaker Heights looking for a party and, for the first time in our high school social lives, actually found one. Unless we know about something going on, we usually end up driving around, wondering where everybody is.

Yesterday (Sunday), was a major, *major* homework day. I had an English paper, a Spanish presentation, and tons of Math homework (which, by the way, remains unfinished). I *literally* spent the whole day doing homework. I only took breaks for brunch (my relatives from Detroit came in so my mom made a nice brunch—bagels with cream cheese and lox, my favorite) and to have dinner with a friend who is home from college. Every time I talk to someone who's already in college, it makes me want to pack up and leave immediately. It was a pretty late night, but since I don't have football, it doesn't really matter. After all that wondering about life after football, I guess it's like when you have a birthday (like turning thirteen or something), and you expect everything to suddenly change because you're older, but nothing really does. Life without football is really just that: life without football.

I'm glad Yale sent me a postcard. I was beginning to worry. I mean, I'm still worried, but now at least I know I'm in their computer. I wish I could fast-forward to December 15 and find out if I'm in or not. If I don't get accepted, I hope I get rejected, not deferred. Being deferred is supposed to be a good thing, since you still have a chance to get in in the spring, but to me it seems like torture—suffering through another four months, waiting for another letter. I've been trying to not get too excited, because I don't want to set myself up for a fall. But I still *really* want to go there as much as I did the first time I saw it. Well, football season worked out well, so I'm one for one in my senior year. Just wrestling, grades, and getting into college to go.

11/7/96—Keep on trucking . . .

I shaved my head. I did the same thing the night before my first football practice and things worked out well, so I'll try it again before wrestling starts tomorrow. The key to this wrestling season is going to be taking things one day at a time. If you think about it as a four-month ordeal, that's what it will be. If you think about it as a collection of separate, two-hour hell sessions, it becomes more manageable in some way. The one potential problem is that I hear from Yale a month into the season. If the news is good, I'll loosen up and probably have a better time and wrestle better. If I don't, then it could be a tough season. Just keep on trucking. (I already told my friends this may be the last "good mood" for a while, so they should consider themselves forewarned.)

►

Alec Berezin
Father

I thought it was great that Josh shaved his head. I mean, shaving it for football practice made all the sense in the world. And he looked awfully good with a shaved head.

11/8/96—Practice was pretty essay (I mean easy) . . .

Well, practice was pretty essay (I mean easy), at least for a wrestling practice. Actually, we didn't wrestle at all, just drilled and did conditioning. One day at a time, and today was a good way to start. When I got home, my parents and I visited a friend of the family in their huge house. I had to answer all the normal college questions, but this time I didn't really mind. I've found that if you keep your head down while you talk it makes things a lot easier. On Sunday night I'm going out with a coworker of my dad's who was a History major at Michigan. She had planned to go pre-med but changed her mind. I think they're going to try to sell me on Michigan. I'm looking forward to hearing what being a History/pre-med major was like. But none of this will matter if I don't *apply*! (Hint to self: Finish Michigan application.)

11/9/96—*I'm not leaving my house tomorrow until it's done . . .*

One of the essays for Michigan is giving me trouble. I don't think they should have two, but it's not really my call. I'm supposed to respond to this statement: "Unique characteristics/qualities you will bring to the UM campus. Explain previous experience and interest in issues related to educational and career goals for the specific school or college to which you are applying. Include any significant leadership experience that you have." Really, that's three different questions (and they're not even questions). I could write a bunch on the first part, but the only experience I have related to my career goals is my volunteer work at the hospital and the time I spent following a few doctors around. My last attempt at a comprehensive answer talks about my unique ability to work well with others, which I noticed was important to doctors during my previous experience relating to my educational and career goals. As you can probably tell, it doesn't make much sense yet. I'm not leaving my house tomorrow until it's done.

Elena called, but she wasn't really calling to ask me to do anything. Or maybe she was, I don't know. I wasn't going anywhere, like I said. Except to take a walk. It snowed like eight inches tonight. It was really beautiful; there was so much snow that power lines and trees were falling over. There's a golf course right behind my building, so I went over the fence and wandered around. I decided to call Elena tomorrow and see if she wants to go sledding. I highly doubt that I will do it, but maybe.

11/10/96—I'm mostly thinking about girls . . .

My excuse for not doing any work on my application today is that I have a day off from school tomorrow. I can't seem to get myself going. I'm bored with school and nervous about wrestling. After tomorrow's practice, we have an awards night for all fall athletes. I'll find out if I made all-league. It would be cool if I did, but I won't get my hopes up.

Dinner with the two Michigan alumni was fun. They were very gung-ho about Ann Arbor, but they were also down-to-earth and easy to talk to. I felt comfortable talking about college with them, which hasn't happened in a while. They just graduated four years ago, though, so I don't consider them to be real adults. And even though the conversation was mostly about Michigan, talking about college made me think about Yale. Is it December 15th yet?

On Friday, one of my friends said I was being very pensive. After the initial shock of hearing the word "pensive" used outside of an English class, I realized that I have been sort of staring off into space thinking about stuff. I'm mostly thinking about girls. Actually one girl in particular: Elena. I'm pretty sure I like her, but not positive. We've been talking on the phone a lot, and I can tell she's liking me more and more as a friend, while I'm liking her more and more as more than a friend. I probably should talk to her about it. (I did call her today, but she was in a bad mood, so I didn't ask her to go sledding with me.) *And* I can't seem to find my applications at the moment. I'm pretty sure they're at school. I don't know what I'd do if I lost them. I guess I would just have to start over from scratch, but that would be a pain in the ass.

11/12/96—Snow day . . .

Snow day! Because of Veterans' Day yesterday, it was our second day off in a row, and they've already canceled tomorrow because the snow's so bad. Snow days are unusual for us; not unusual like once or twice a year, but like we went 17 years without one. But we have almost two feet of snow right now, and it's really unbelievable.

Wrestling practice has also been canceled for the past two days, but I'm sure we will have it tomorrow. It will be the first real day of practice. On Monday they canceled the fall sports awards banquet, too, so I don't know if I'm all-league or not. And today I got invited to attend a panel on Yale, which will be hosted by the lady who is reviewing my application. It's on the 26th, so I assume she'll have some idea about my status. I'm a little nervous about it, but I don't know why.

At least I've got a chance to catch up with my work. I finally finished my Michigan essay. Here it is:

Topic 1: Unique Characteristics and Previous Experiences Relating to Career Goals

When I was seven years old, my sister threw a Frisbee straight up into the air, and it came down straight on my head. Enraged and with a bump on my noggin, I chased her all around the yard seeking revenge. I finally cornered her in my garage, and tried to hit her like she had never been hit before. Unfortunately, I missed her face and punched my hand through a glass door. When I got to the emergency room, the doctor cleaned me up, calmed me down, and stitched my arm up. I'm much less violent now, but that event continues to have an effect on my life. First, my sister still refuses to toss the Frisbee around with me. More important though, that event spurred in me an interest in medicine. Ever since then, I've known that I have wanted to become a doctor, just like the one who treated me.

Over the past four years, I have tried to gain as much experience as possible in medical-related fields. Over the summer following my sophomore year, I volunteered at a local hospital, helping sick children cope with hospitalization. Last summer I spent time shadowing two doctors. The first was a neonatalogist. He let me make rounds with him and his staff. This was only a one-day experience, but I learned a great deal. The experience with the second doctor was equally educational and even more exciting. I spent an entire week with an emergency room physician, watching him treat everything from pneumonia to cardiac arrest. Besides these hands-on experiences, I also have watched many medical procedures on television and read about the changes in the field of medicine in newspapers and magazines.

While following doctors around, watching an operation on TV, or spending time with sick kids, I have noticed that doctors need to have the ability to relate well to people as well as the ability to work well in a team. I believe that I possess these abilities. I have participated in many group-oriented activities, ranging from a three-week Outward Bound program in the mountains of North Carolina, to playing high school football. Through these activities, I have learned how to work and succeed with people from different ethnic, cultural, and economic backgrounds.

My experiences as the captain of my football team are probably the best example of how well I work with people. The high school I attend boasts that it has achieved a truly integrated environment. In the classrooms, hallways, and cafeteria, though, people are sharply separated along racial lines. One exception to this situation is the football team. The majority of the kids on the team are African-American, and the rest of the kids are white. Some of the players, like myself, are also Jewish. Over the past four years, I have played with and befriended people from all walks of life. I have learned that people have different ways of looking at situations, because of their different backgrounds. Once you understand where people are coming from, you can work with them on a team.

Besides helping me to achieve my career goals, I think that my ability to get along with people is something unique that I can contribute to the University of Michigan. A large university, Michigan obviously attracts a diverse student body. I feel that since I can relate well to different people, I will be able to fully take advantage of the people and opportunities that the University of Michigan has to offer.

►

Rachael
Sister

That Frisbee incident was Josh's fault. He was trying to punch me when he hit the glass door. I didn't know it was so important to him, though.

11/14/96—Yes, they take plastic . . .

I finally turned in my Michigan application, but not without a hitch. My dad forgot to give me the check for the application fee before he and my mom left for Santa Fe. I had a momentary panic attack, but it'll be okay. I talked to my parents and I'll either forge a check (this is the worst-case scenario—is it a felony to forge a check?), or just give them my mom's MasterCard number. Yes, they take plastic.

I found out this morning that my Economics teacher has cancer. She's one of the nicest people and it's a little upsetting. She plans to come to school even when she's on radiation. That should be a dose of perspective for me. I really feel bad for her, but I think that if anyone can pull through, she can.

My English teacher assigned three poems for class tomorrow. Why do English teachers make you write poetry? Isn't the point to express your emotions, not fake them? I ended up writing one about a beetle (yes, the insect—that bee topic wasn't actually too far off), one about my messy room and my trophies, and one about a rabbi. That last one is actually pretty good.

11/17/96—Red tape at the guidance office . . .

I put my mom's credit card number on the application, but not until I went through all the red tape at the guidance office. First, I had to tell the lady who sends out the final applications that I had the credit card number. She, not surprisingly, didn't have the application anymore. She had given it to Mrs. Blattner, who was in a meeting with a parent at the time. I was about to leave the office when I saw *my* application in Mrs. Blattner's mailbox. So I took out the application and I'm writing the credit card number on it when this lady starts yelling at me about how I can't do that because blah blah *blah* blah *blah*, and I should be *shot* for committing such a *grievous* error. Now I have no idea if she'll even send it out. You know, as punishment.

Friday night after practice I went to the pool to see Elena dive. This was the first time I had ever witnessed her doing this and she completely fucked up. It was one of the funniest things I have ever seen. She was sweet in the air, but she landed flat on her face. I shouldn't laugh, because it probably hurt a lot. She was embarrassed when she saw me, and she came over to talk. I told her to call me, which she did. She called once early in the evening just to see what I was doing and then again at 11 to talk about how her parents were annoying her. Every time I talk to her, I start thinking that she's interested in me, but I can't quite bring myself to bring it up. I don't even know if I like her or not. I'm definitely physically attracted to her, and I'm already friends with her. Well, whatever—she said she'd call me on Saturday, and I figured we'd go out.

Saturday morning's scrimmage was tough. I'm really out of shape. I went out for lunch with Aaron, got home, turned on the TV, and literally waited by the phone. No dice. So instead of salvaging the evening—going out or working on my massive pile of homework—I watched TV, felt sorry for myself, ate ten waffles in under 20 minutes, and worried about college. (By the way, I got a letter from Yale telling me my interviewer will contact me soon and inviting me again to an information conference on the 26th. I can't wait to get interviewed and get this whole thing over with.) The only homework I did was read some of *Crime and Punishment*, which is not the best book to read to lift your spirits. So I went to bed, figuring if Elena was interested, she would call and we'd get together. After all, she knew that I was at home alone and that I wanted to see her. But she didn't call, so I figured once and for all that she wasn't interested. It's disappointing but at least it's an answer. So this morning (Sunday), I got up to do some homework, and actually got some work done.

Then who should call but Elena. She wanted to come over and study. So I said yes. Of course. What's the matter with me? When she got here, she saw the mess in my room and helped me clean up a little. We went to buy my mom a birthday present. (I got her a nice bracelet, hope she likes it.) We worked for maybe ten minutes when we got home, until she got frustrated with studying and turned on the TV. A prolonged wrestling match for the remote control ensued, which involved her hiding it in her pants and me going after it, among other things. It was really nothing serious, but it was one of those moments when, even though you're just laughing and fooling around, you feel like you're on the brink of something. But even when she was all over me, and I was all over her, I *still* didn't make a move. I've got to tell her how I feel eventually, although if she doesn't know by this point, she's not too bright. I wish I wasn't so shy with girls; hopefully it will be different in college. Really, it's more like nervous than shy. Well, maybe I'll talk to her about it tomorrow. I've got so much work to catch up on, though, I'm not sure if I'll have time to call her. Wrestling's going to be tough tomorrow also, so I'll be pretty tired and very grouchy.

►

Elena
The Girl from Spanish Class

The more I got to know Josh, the more I liked him. I knew what was going on—that he liked me. He's a really funny guy. Like, he never calls anybody—he always waits for people to call him and ask him to go out. So I started taking him out to parties and stuff.

11/20/96—Mrs. Blattner told me not to kill myself . . .

I am swamped. I had an English test on Monday, a Physics test on Tuesday, another English test, and an Economics test today

(Wednesday). The only one I've gotten back so far is Physics, and it wasn't pretty: 40 percent. There goes any hope of a good grade in that class. (Actually not, 'cause I can retake it, but what's the likelihood of that happening?) I'm starting to come down with a major case of senioritis, or should I say Yale-itis. I just really don't *care* that much about high school right now. My mind's already halfway to Connecticut. My workload will ease up after today, but this weekend is really busy. They postponed that fall sports thing till tomorrow because of the snow, and I've got a community service project on Friday night, and early Saturday morning I have to help Terrell Brandon (who plays for the Cavs) and Aaron's father (who is a reverend) give turkeys to needy families, *and* go to wrestling practice at 8:00 A.M. on Saturday, *and* go to the football banquet on Sunday. Tuesday I have this forum on Yale, and Wednesday I have my interview. Yes, that's right, I scheduled my interview. The guy seemed nice. He's coming here, so that means I have exactly one week to clean up. That should be enough, but I'll have to get cracking. I'm actually not too nervous about the interview. We'll be at home, where I'm comfortable, and we'll just talk for an hour. I'm also—for the moment—not too worried about getting into Yale on December 15. This is probably a very bad thing, but I have a good feeling about it. Though I'm trying as hard as I can not to set myself up for a monstrous fall. I've got to get moving—most of the schools want form one (the one that just asks for my name, and school and family information and stuff) and the fee A.S.A.P. Mrs. Blattner said not to kill myself to get them done, though. Either way, I'd like to get them done with. I also have to call Michigan to make sure they received all of my stuff.

Wrestling has been tough because I'm not in good shape. There's a huge difference between football shape and wrestling shape. One day at a time.

11/21/96—I got shafted . . .

I didn't make all-league in football. I'm not really that mad about it, even though I got shafted. What happened, according to my coach, is that since all of the other offensive lineman were all-league, the other coaches didn't want to give all the awards to one team, so I was the odd man out. I did share an award for Outstanding Offensive Lineman for the team, which means a lot to me. Tomorrow and Saturday I have that community service thing. It should be fun. I also have tons and tons of homework, so it's good times all around.

11/24/96—My football career is officially over . . .

The annual football awards banquet was a great time. All of the seniors get to roast the coaches (I did Coach Sedmak), and everyone was hilarious. So my football career is officially over as of right now. Once I give it a second thought I know that I'll have wonderful memories. Do I miss it already?

The community service work I did over the weekend was a good time. Terrell Brandon didn't show, but it was still fun. Friday night Aaron and I went to a high school hockey game. Hockey games get the biggest, nosiest, drunkest crowds, so it was very entertaining. I saw Elena there but didn't make any effort to talk to her. Saturday I locked myself in a room, did Math homework for six hours, and I still am not even close to finishing. Well, close maybe, but I certainly don't understand any of it.

My biggest worry right now is that I won't get into Yale, although I still have that nagging good feeling. (I really have to work on my other applications over the Thanksgiving weekend.) I keep on thinking that if I don't get in, I'll have to explain what happened to every person who knows I applied there. It'll be really embarrassing—not to mention heartbreaking. Still, it would be worth it to know I gave it my best shot.

11/25/96—I can't decide what to say . . .

Wrestling was tough today. I've been trying not to think about it outside of practice for fear it would be depressing, but it's actually going really well. Maybe "really well" is too strong—I could be working just a bit harder.

Tomorrow I have this conference on Yale. I can't decide what to say. It wouldn't matter except I've already made such a fool of myself in front of Tamara Shirdak. Should I just go up and say hello and hope she remembers me, or ask her about Yale's swimming pool, or what? I've asked her dumb questions once, and I don't want to do it again. (I'm being a bit anal here, I realize.) December 15 is looming large on the calendar. I'm not really counting the days, but I am already checking the mail. I *am* setting myself up to be let down, but I can't help myself.

11/26/96—"Yale is great, Yale is good" . . .

The Yale conference was fairly informative. There was a panel of current students there with Tamara Shirdak. It lasted about two hours and consisted of the normal "Yale is great, Yale is good" stuff, but they were also very up front about drinking and other usually ignored issues. I got the impression once again that Yale is a place where smart people enjoy arguing as much as I do—about everything from food to poverty. A recent Yale graduate who was on the panel is now a lawyer in Cleveland. My dad had heard of him and talked to him for a while after the conference was over. Turns out he played football at Yale. He was about my size, although he played safety instead of center. Dad introduced us and the guy was very polite. He said everyone told him he was too small, but he really thought he could play there, so he called the athletic department and told them about himself. He thinks it helped him get in. . . . I think I can't handle thinking about football right now.

11/27/96—Medicine and all that jazz . . .

My Yale interview wasn't bad at all. Actually, I had a pretty good time. The guy, who's a Yale alumnus, came over at about eight, and we just chatted for a while about how I became interested in Yale, what I planned to study, et cetera, et cetera. We talked about why I wanted to be a doctor, what I've done to pursue my interests in medicine and all that jazz. He was extremely easy to talk to and I felt really comfortable the whole time. After about an hour, my parents and my sister came home from dinner (I made them go out so we would have some privacy), and we all talked for another 45 minutes. He told us some funny stories about himself, talked about what it was like being a lawyer, gave me his phone number, and left. He stayed for two hours, so I assume he enjoyed himself. I really don't know exactly what it did for me in terms of admissions, but it could only have helped. Oh, yeah, we also talked about literature and books I like, but I failed to mention my journal project. I was going to, but it never really came up.

11/30/96—Pleasant is about the only word . . .

I got into college. I've been checking the mail regularly now, even though I know I'm not supposed to hear from Yale for another two weeks. I wasn't really expecting to hear from Michigan for at least another month, but it was a pleasant surprise, to find my acceptance letter in the mailbox yesterday. And pleasant is about the only word to describe it. Not thrilled, not overjoyed, just pleased. I thought that I would be much more excited about it. I mean, I'm excited, I'm just not jumping up and down for joy.

Last night I went to the movies with my friend Alex. (He's at Ohio University and is back for six weeks. Everyone says that your friends change when they go to college, but last night was really just like old times.) I slept in until about noon today, which was nice. I lost a wrestling match tonight, but it was to someone better than just about everyone, and I wrestled pretty well. I still have so much work to do, but I can't find any motivation. I hope I don't get deferred from Yale, because once they get my semester grades, my stock may plummet, so to speak.

I talked to Elena on Friday night. She called and asked me what I was doing. I of course said nothing, hoping that she would reply "Oh, let's go out." Nope. She had plans with her best friend's ex-boyfriend, or something to that effect. I said if those plans fell through, she should call me so we could do something. So, in a manner of speaking, I actually asked her out. My dad made fun of me for not just asking her outright—a good example of why I try very hard to keep my parents out of my social life.

My sister is home on winter break, and we got into a big fight over phone usage. She said I was having a steroid rage and I called her a selfish bitch. It's times like these when you realize how much you love someone.

12/1/96—Now I understand why I don't give a damn . . .

Now I understand why I don't give a damn about high school anymore. Because I know my grades will work out—they always do. But my applications aren't going to get done by themselves.

I need to be working on them and, for some strange reason, I'm just not. They're just sitting there. I'm hoping that eventually (preferably before the due date), I will be inspired to finish them.

12/2/96—Some great revelation . . .

I'm almost done with my Columbia application. What made me get motivated again? Some flash of desire? Some great revelation about the nature of college? No, it was the deadline.

In school today my Spanish teacher commented that I seemed a bit down. I told him I was just a little bored with everything and he understood. It was nice to have a teacher actually voice a concern for me, so I feel obligated to work a little harder in his class. That was probably his plan.

12/4/96—The guidance office is going to bust my balls . . .

I am by far the stupidest person that I have ever met. How else would you explain the fact that I had absolutely no idea when my Stanford application was due? I, being the idiot that I am, thought that it was due on January 1, like all of my other applications. Well, it's not. It's due on the December 15. That might not seem that bad, but even if I finish everything else, I can't get it typed until Sunday, and the guidance office is going to bust my balls because you're supposed to have everything in three weeks before the due date. I already might have to ask them for some extra time with my other applications. It's not like I didn't have time, I could have done the application a long time ago if I hadn't been so *stupid*. Maybe Yale will mail me an acceptance tomorrow, even though that would be two weeks early. (With the way things are going, it would probably be a rejection with a note saying "We couldn't figure out if you were for real. Thanks for all the laughs you provided us during our application review meetings.")

12/6/96—What can you do?

Tonight I had the choice of finishing up my college applications (Stanford has to be done by Sunday) or going to the school play. I consulted some of my friends, and the decision was unanimous: Go to the play. So I went and it was really unbelievable. It was a production of *Guys and Dolls*, and they did it really well. I've always been a bit jealous of actors because they get to go on stage and be "the man" for a while, but tonight I really wished I was part of the show. I'll just do my applications tomorrow night after I get home from the wrestling tournament. (It will be my first real match of the year and I'm competing four times tomorrow so I know I'll be real exhausted but what can you do? I've always known that it would come down to the last possible moment.)

12/7/96—I have to go to bed right now . . .

It's about 2 A.M. I just finished my Stanford application, and it is not very good. I'll explain everything tomorrow, but I have to go to bed right now.

12/8/96—Say good-bye to my love handles . . .

Okay, here's what's going on. At 7:30 yesterday morning (Saturday), I woke up to go to a wrestling tournament. My first match was at 10:30, and I lost to a kid who wasn't very good. All of my feelings of self-doubt and embarrassment from last year came back, and I was quite depressed. I talked to my coach about it, and he just kept telling me he thought I was going to have a great year and he knows that I am a good wrestler. Now I just have to start believing what he said.

My next match was against a tough kid from Warrensville who's a quality wrestler. I lost to him also, but I could deal with that one. I wrestled a good smart match and only lost by a few points. The other two matches (today's and one last week) I got forfeits. So technically, I'm 3–2, but I haven't really won a match yet. I know it will happen, but I'm not sure when and against whom. Aaron took first, though, with another kid from our team, and yet another took second.

Coach called me today and told me that he thought I was wrestling well but that I was just too small for 189 pounds (my weight class). We agreed I would try to lose the 18 pounds to make 171. It seems like a lot to lose in a month, but it's really not that much. I have to say good-bye to my love handles though.

By the time I got home, it was 11 o'clock. I had already read the Stanford application and figured that I could finish it in about an hour. So four hours later I finally finished the thing. They asked the stupidest questions. One was about an activity, one was about an intellectually exciting person, and one was supposed to be a note to your future college roommate about an experience that helped shape your life. I wrote about football for the question about an activity. Here's what I said:

Question Number One—An Activity

Of all the activities, interests, and experiences listed above, football is the most meaningful to me. When I started high school I was a pudgy, dorky little kid who never did homework and watched about seven hours of television a day. Around the middle of my freshman year, I made a decision to dedicate myself completely to football for the rest of my high school career. I attended workouts, both in the off season and the in season, for three years, rarely missing a workout and never missing a practice. By participating in high school football, I have become a physically and mentally stronger person with a clear set of goals and the motivation necessary to achieve those goals.

Question Number Two—An Intellectually Stimulating Person

I loved going to second period last year. I would walk in to that class exhausted from a late night of studying and leave practically jumping off the walls. What caused this miraculous transformation was 45 minutes of listening to Mr. Pollack's annoying, nasal voice. Mr. Pollack was my U.S. History teacher last year, and he was one of the most intellectually exciting people I have ever met. He had a well of knowledge so deep that he could have taught five periods a day, five days a week, all four years of high school, and he would still have lessons left untaught. What made Mr. Pollack so exciting, though, was not so much what he taught but the way that he taught it. Mr. Pollack was so enthusiastic about teaching his students not to recite names and dates but how to think analytically and how to back up arguments with facts. Mr. Pollack woke me up every morning by forcing me to think about what I was saying and how I was saying it. I cannot think of anything more intellectually exciting than using your mind to create clear, concise, and practically irrefutable arguments.

Question Number Three—Note About an Experience That Changed Your Life

David,

Last year's wrestling season was one of the most difficult

times in my life. I had to wrestle Junior Varsity as a junior. That may not seem like much, but if you had to explain to all of your friends and family that you couldn't make the cut, then I think you would understand. I struggled through it, though. It was embarrassing, painful, and depressing, but I made it. I stared adversity in the face, and I did not let it defeat me. I think about last year's season every day of my life, and it always reminds me to never give up.

Okay, so it's cheesy, but it was three in the morning.

Then I had to write a one-page essay about a photograph that had some special meaning to me and then explain its significance. The essay actually turned out pretty good, the picture was of me playing football.

Time comes to a grinding halt. Teeth clenched, muscles churning, your senses become keen. You can hear every breath, every grunt, every groan. You can even smell your opponents sweat. You spot your adversary out of the corner of your eye: number 59. You see that he is bigger than you, but you have no fear. You smash your helmet into his chest, like a ramrod breaking down a door. Your arms extend, tossing him to the ground in a moment of sheer ecstasy. Although it lasts only a fraction of a second, the hit seems like an eternity. When the whistle blows, time speeds up again. You see your opponent on the ground, and you know you have won the battle.

This photo captures one of the many times that I had this experience, but it does not tell the whole story. It does not explain why this seemingly insignificant event means so much to me. What cannot be seen in the photo are the countless years of preparation. There is no hint of the literally thousands of sprints that I have run, or of the tons of weights I have lifted, or of the long practices that I have endured. Even the least-informed football fan can see that this play is perfect. My teammates and I have opened up a hole the size of a Mack truck for the back to run through, but there is no way to see the countless times we practiced this play until it was absolutely flawless. You can see the coaches in the lower-right-hand corner, but you cannot hear them screaming at the offensive line to "hold those blocks." And where in this photo is there any indication of the grueling, 100-degree-eight-hours-a-day-starting-at-seven-o'clock-summer-practices that we survived? You can see other players on the field, but you cannot possibly know about all the hilarious locker room jokes we told, or the times we supported each other when one of us was down.

This picture represents the culmination of the years of teamwork, dedication, and perseverance. All of the work, the sprints, the weights, the practices, everything, it all merged into an electric ball of energy that I released in the half second it took to put number 59 on his butt. And I knew during this half second that my fellow offensive lineman were also doing their jobs and that the back would make the right cut. (By the way, we scored on this play, and won the game by 30 points.) This picture also shows something that I am extremely proud of, my size. Normally, being short is a source of embarrassment, but it gives me a sense of pride. I am 5 foot 8, weigh 200 pounds after a big meal, and I started twenty games on an offensive line that averaged 6 foot 2 and 270 pounds. That is one of the reasons that I worked as hard as I did, and it made it all the more meaningful when I knocked a kid who outweighed me by 50 pounds, like number 59, to the grass. Football was the most meaningful thing

I did during high school, and I think this photograph, along with all of the work that went into the moment that it captures, demonstrates why football was so important to me.

I actually did the essay today because it did not have to be typed on the form. I just pasted it on. So this morning my poor father went in to the office to type the rest of the application up. I was glad to have it done even if it did take me all night.

By the way, at some point during the past week, I did my application to Columbia. I gave it to my dad tonight so he could type it tomorrow. So four down, two to go. At this point, I think that if I only got in to Penn and Michigan, I would go to Michigan, so I'm not exactly sure why I'm killing myself to complete the Penn application on time. By the way, I have no idea how or when my applications are going to be sent. As I've explained before, my guidance office asks that you turn in your applications three weeks before they are due. So I guess Stanford is getting to California just a little bit late. I'll have to kiss some ass in the guidance office to make sure they get out on time. Also, since I applied early to Yale, they will hold my other applications, all of which are due on January 1, so if by some off-chance I *do* get into Yale, I won't have wasted my money on unnecessary application fees. So my question is, when should I have those three applications in to the guidance office? I think the reason they need them three weeks early is to give them time to do the counselor recommendations, and I have already given Mrs. Blattner all the forms but Penn's, so I should be in good shape. I hope.

I have to talk with Mrs. Blattner about this stuff tomorrow, although I don't know how much it will help me figure it out. I always leave her office more confused than when I came in. I am so ready to be done with this. Meanwhile, if I get into Yale, all this last-minute rushing around will be for naught. Which reminds me, I am nervous about Yale—just a touch, but enough so that the good gut feeling I had is gone, replaced by butterflies. I come home every day to check the mail even though I heard the admissions director say they were sending the responses out on the 11th. If I called right now, they probably could tell me my status, but I just can't do it. I'm really very stressed about the whole thing, and it would make my day (year, life, existence!) to get into college and concentrate on having a good senior year. Ugh.

12/9/96—They are stupid and mean people . . .

I WANT MY LETTER FROM YALE AND I WANT IT RIGHT NOW. I KNOW THAT THEY HAVE THEM DONE. WHY DON'T THEY JUST SEND THE STUPID LETTERS? THEY ARE CAUSING A GREAT DEAL OF STRESS. THEY ARE STUPID AND MEAN PEOPLE. I BETTER GET MY LETTER TOMORROW.

▶

Mr. Pollack
Eleventh-Grade History Teacher

There's tremendous frustration surrounding the college process, there's no doubt about that. There are a lot of kids who allow the stress to overcome them. As a teacher, you separate yourself from that. You hope for the best for the kids, and you hope their dreams are fulfilled.

I don't think it's healthy. I think that any school can be the best school if a student wants it to be, and kids can overcome colleges that they feel are inadequate. What the application process does is put the stress on the college rather than on learning. And then on grades rather than learning, and on competition rather than learning. We're here to help kids grow and mature and learn, but this process often detracts from what we do.

12/10/96—That about sums it up . . .

I'm wrestling like shit, not doing any homework, not working on college applications. But I *am* talking on the phone and watching television a lot. That about sums it up. I wish that letter would come.

12/11/96—I might be completely miserable for another three months . . .

This is getting ridiculous. I am really in a rut, and I don't even know why. I guess it is just a combination of all the crap (wrestling, grades, cutting weight, girls) and the huge knot in my stomach about Yale. I'm being terribly mean to everyone I know, although I am trying to give them some fair warning. I e-mailed Yale asking them when the letters were going out and apparently the magic date is Friday the 13th. So I have to wait at least another five days. Anyway, I hope things start to pick up, otherwise I could be completely miserable for at least another three months.

Yesterday Elena and I talked about Prom. No, I didn't ask her or anything, it just came up. I've heard the word "Prom" like 20 times in the past week; everyone's obsessed, from strangers in the hall to my Economics teacher. (We were talking about how I was going to find a Prom date if I didn't cut my hair.) So somehow when I'm talking to Elena, Prom comes up and she starts telling me about her ideal Prom night. Being the idiot that I am, I, of course, suggested that I might want to get it on with my date on

Prom night, if you know what I mean. She was kind of appalled and blew the whole thing way out of proportion. She lectured me about how surprised she was that I would say that, and how sex should be about love and all that stuff. But, really, that's what I was saying. The way I always pictured it, I would have a serious girlfriend all senior year and Prom would be the big night. So, really, I had thought about it in basically the same terms she had. It sounded like she had done some thinking on the subjects of Prom and love and sex—though I couldn't tell if good ol' Josh was involved in that thought process, too. If I was, I'm definitely not anymore after saying that I want to get laid by my date to a girl who thinks the way she does. Great.

►

Elena
The Girl from Spanish Class

One time on the phone, I asked Josh if he wanted to have sex on Prom night. I was curious. And he was like, yeah—with you. I got really mad. I thought, how dare you! What if it was just a one-night thing? He shouldn't expect anything like that. I was really mad.

12/12/96—A letter that could change my life . . .

I heard from my sister's friend's mother again, the one whose son is now at Yale (my sister's friend's brother, that is); she called to wish me luck. She also said that some of the guidance counselors and my principal probably already know but won't tell me. It was very nice of her to call. Besides that interesting event, I've just been twiddling my thumbs till Monday rolls around . . . doing very little schoolwork. I think getting into Yale would give me a boost that could carry me at least through the end of first semester. If I get deferred or denied, then I *have* to do well, or else I might not get in anywhere else.

My second wrestling tournament of the season is tomorrow. I really don't feel good about the way I've been wrestling or about my attitude in general. My coach keeps telling me I'm doing well, but if I'm not winning matches, it's kind of hard to believe. My goal for tomorrow is to place in this tournament. I deserve it.

►

Coach Kornblut
Wrestling Coach

I gave Josh some advice about getting into Yale. I told him to lie. I said the admissions process can be ridiculous and you need to stand out from the crowd. Make something up. Make something up that's absolutely outrageous and they'll be more likely to go for it. Here he was busting his butt trying to do everything possible. So when I talked to him, I suggested he say that he had a job as a chef in a Chinese restaurant. I thought he should say that he worked as a busboy and that one day the chef didn't show up and that he took over and saved the day and that he became a chef in a Chinese restaurant. I thought that sort of thing would get their attention.

I said what you need to do is keep in mind that you're doing your absolute best. If it's good enough to get into Yale, terrific, if it's not, it's their loss. That was my feeling about it.

12/14/96—I guess I thought wrong . . .

This weekend did not go well at all. I left school at 1:00 on Friday to go to my tournament, got there, weighed in (still at 189), and waited about four hours to wrestle. I thought that I was prepared mentally, but I guess I thought wrong. I lost my second match by one point to the kid who took fourth place. I scored points in the last few seconds, but there was a problem with the clock and somehow I ended up losing. I wasn't too upset about it because I really thought I still had a chance to do well in the tournament. Again I thought wrong. I lost to a kid whom I could have and should have beaten easily. After *that* match I was upset. My coach gave me a little pep talk. He said that he thought I was a great kid and a really hard worker and that I would come out on top if I persevered. I couldn't even look him in the eye. I can't look anyone in the eye right now. I'm embarrassed to go out there and lose all the time. I'm going to cut to 171 pounds—maybe that will help.

I came home from the tournament prepared for a rejection from Yale. Luckily it wasn't there, so I guess I have to wait until Monday to be let down. Right now I don't even know if getting in would make me happy. I'm going for a jog.

12/15/96—Either way, I'll be okay . . .

So this is it. Tomorrow I find out. Either way, I'll be okay, though okay is certainly relative. We have tomorrow off from wrestling so I'll be able to come straight home after school for the mail. I've been doing some thinking, getting things cleared up in my head. I don't want to write anything more until I work it all out.

Part Four

▶

The Final
Moments

12/16/96
2:20 P.M.—I'm just going to sit here and wait . . .

December 16. I should be getting an important piece of mail today. It is 2:20 in the afternoon and I don't have wrestling practice, so I'm just going to sit here and wait until the stupid, lazy-ass mailman comes. This is too much.

2:30 P.M.—Go figure . . .

The mailman is here, but he is doing the other side of my apartment building first. Perfect. I suppose that there is no use in asking him if he could move it along a bit and get to the important stuff. Just a few more minutes. I know I am going to get deferred; it would just make sense that after months of tortured worrying and waiting, I will be greeted with a letter asking me to wait for another three months.

2:35 P.M.—I gfot ion!

I got ion IO g ot uin hell yeah i am going to Yale ia got in I gfot ion! I can't believe that I am going to Yale. Let me say that again, I am going to Yale! I have tons of homework to do tonight, but who the hell really cares!!!! I waited outside the mailroom until the mailman was finished with all of the mail. I just walked in and opened our box. I knew that if waited too long, I would freeze up and end up standing there like an asshole for a half hour. I opened the box, and there were two magazines and a thick envelope in between. I looked under the bottom magazine nothing there. Then I slowly lifted up the top magazine, and I saw that the letter was fat and that it was from Yale. I ripped it open, and there was a cardboard thing that said "Welcome to Yale." Inside was my acceptance letter and the terms of agreement (my acceptance of their acceptance, basically). I read only far enough to know I had actually gotten in and then I went crazy. I started jumping all over the place and screaming and yelling. I ran back to my apartment and called my mom, who wasn't there. I left a message saying "I got in!" and figured she would know what I was talking about. I knew my dad was in a deposition and I wouldn't be able to reach him. So I called my sister who was very excited and then called my aunt and uncle and they went crazy, too. Then I ran out to my car and drove to school to tell all of my teachers. I almost got in three accidents because I was so excited. My football coach wasn't there so I immediately went up to the guidance office to tell Mrs. Blattner. She was in a meeting. I went on to this other room in the office and asked another counselor where she was. This counselor knew who I was and asked if I got in, so I threw down my acceptance packet on the table, and she went crazy. She jumped up and down and gave me a hug. While I was waiting for Mrs. Blattner, I went around and found a few of my teachers who had helped me with my applications. I located only a few of them but, as expected, they went crazy. Everyone was going crazy, I can't think of any other word to describe it. After about an hour I finally found Mrs. Blattner and told her the good news. She was beyond crazy, she was ecstatic. This may have been the best day of my life. We talked a while about how happy I was and how great this was, and then I left school to go home and call my parents. I got hold of my dad. He had already heard the message from Mom, but he wasn't positive, so when I told him, he was out of control. We called my mom on conference call and talked for a while about how unbelievable it all was.

►

Marcia Berezin
Mother

I was pretty calm in the morning on the day Josh was supposed to hear from Yale. But I had an approximate idea of when the mail was going to come, and when that time came I was testing someone's hearing, but the poor person was not getting my undivided attention, I'm afraid. As the minutes were ticking by, I was looking at my watch and thinking, "I haven't heard from him, I haven't heard from him." I just thought to myself, "Oh, please, please let him get in." I knew how badly he wanted it and I wanted it for him.

And then I got a message on my door that said "Josh called. He got in." But the person who took the message is, as my son would say, not the sharpest crayon in the box, so I wasn't quite sure whether I should believe her or not. I dashed to the phone to try and get Josh but I couldn't get ahold of him. So I called Alec thinking that he would have had the straight scoop, but he didn't. Finally I got in touch with my brother, Kenny, who had actually spoken with Josh, and then I knew that he had got in. I was really excited. It was fantastic. I eventually did get ahold of Josh and he was on air. That's the only way to describe it.

►

Alec Berezin
Father

I don't know if I was at a deposition that day or what, but when I got back from wherever I was, I had a message from Marcia's office that said "Josh got in." The people at Marcia's office are idiots so I just wasn't sure what was going on. So I tried to call Marcia and Uncle Kenny and didn't get either of them. I was getting a little crazy, trying to find Mrs. Blattner or someone else at the school who knew. I couldn't get through. I was beside myself. Josh finally called me and said he got in. I just went crazy. I started to cry. I went out of control. Everybody in my office knew within 30 seconds. Driving home, I stopped at a stoplight, rolled down my window, and told everyone—I was really obnoxious. But I was just overjoyed.

After I spoke with my parents, I started calling a bunch of friends and relatives. Shellie got into Harvard, along with another kid. Three people got into Princeton, and a bunch got into Emory. I talked to almost everyone I knew and then people who had heard started calling out of the blue. There aren't words to describe how happy and excited I am right now, although orgasmic comes to mind. Everything, all the hours of studying, all of the stress, all of the delayed gratification, it was all worth it for today. I do have some homework to do, so I can't keep on writing, but I know I won't forget anything.

And Coach Kornblut called. He was really excited for me. He said all weekend he was hoping I would get in, because he knew if I got rejected, he would have to keep me away from sharp objects after my depression this past weekend. I'm completely overwhelmed right now. My parents are calling everyone they have ever met. I really don't mean to gloat about it, but at the same time, I want to tell my friends the good news. All of the people whom I called have been excited for me—my friend Lindsey even started to cry. I called Elena, and we postponed an argument (over what I don't know) until tomorrow. I called my aunts, my cousins, my friends' parents, my sister's friends' parents, my parents' friends, my friends. Tomorrow I'm going to try to wake up a little earlier and get to school in time to tell my football coach and the two teachers who worked on my recommendations.

When I went by the school this afternoon, I was telling one of my teachers when my friend walked by and asked what was wrong with me—presumably because I was bright red and shaking all over. The teacher said, "Josh got into Yale, do you believe it?" I have a feeling everyone will know by tomorrow, and I can't say that I mind. I have to be careful not to slack off, because that could ruin the rest of my year. I've got to try to be humble.

Here is list of people who know the good news: Sheryll was really excited, Aunty Judy was really excited, Leslie, Schuyler, Bryan, Shellie, Sara, Mrs. Jones, Mrs. Kelly, Mrs. Blair, Uncle Kenny, Aunt Debbie, Aunt Lenore, Barbara Brody, the Kalettes, Coach Kornblut, the guidance office, almost everyone in my dad's office (and probably his whole building), and probably some others whom I am forgetting. I know there is so much more to say, but I am exhausted and must go to bed.

►

Mrs. Blattner
Guidance Counselor

The day Josh got his acceptance letter was unbelievable. I was actually cofacilitating a meeting when there was a knock on my door. One of the other counselors had come to get me. She said, you've got to get over here right away. That smile stretched from the top of Josh's face to the bottom of his chin. It was unbelievable. He gave me this great big bear hug and he was just absolutely dancing around. I was ecstatic. I really was. He was just about crying. And he had everybody else in the office jumping and dancing. Everybody loves Josh.

12/17/96—The talk of the school . . .

Today was one of the best days of school ever. I was the man today. Everyone knew about Yale, I got congratulated by about 50 people, and some of my friends are just as excited about the whole thing as I am. I told my two teachers who wrote my recommendations, and they were both wild. One of them told me to start my senior slump the second I got home today. (I did my best but I still did some homework.) Mr. Rankin told me awhile ago that if I got into Yale, I would have to take him out to dinner. I walked into his room and said: "You remember that deal we had about me taking you out to dinner if I got into Yale? Where do you want to go?" He smiled and congratulated me—and then said he wanted Chinese food. I told him I would appreciate it if we could postpone our meal until after wrestling season, though, since I would like to join him in eating. My football coach was equally happy for me. This is a really great feeling.

My dad is telling so many people, it's sick. All of my relatives know, and a bunch of my cousins have called. He keeps on telling strangers about it. For instance, today he overheard two lawyers discussing the cost of college and they were talking about how there were only three or four schools that would be worth the cost of sending your kid out of state: Harvard, Yale . . . Immediately after Yale was mentioned, my dad jumped in and said, "I'm glad you said that 'cause my kid just got in there yesterday." They went crazy, high-fiving him and everything. I feel so relaxed. I decided that from now on I'm not going to tell anyone unless they ask. Well, if they don't know from the huge smile on my face, they'll figure it out. Four people came up to me and said I was the talk of the school. Finally everything paid off. I can't wait to go to family events now, where I used to dread having to talk about college. Now I can tell them where I am going and tell them with pride.

I have to notify Stanford that I'm canceling my application, so I'll write that letter right now. I immediately tore up my other applications after I got the letter. I thought I would really be excited about not having to do any more work, or worry about college anymore, but it turns out I'm excited because I AM GOING TO YALE!!!!!!!!!!

EPILOGUE
▶

7/21/97

So, seven months after receiving that life-changing letter, much of my life remains the same. The rest of first semester went fine for me, I got all As (save for a B in Spanish—I think I have Elena to thank for that one), and despite being a second-semester senior already accepted to college, I managed to avoid a major case of senioritis, ending the year with all As (save for a B in Physics for which I have only myself to blame). But don't think I worked too hard second semester, not by any stretch of the imagination. I just did all of my major assignments the night (or morning) before they were due.

Graduation was fun. The heavens opened in celebration and presented us with a torrential downpour during the first five minutes of the ceremony, which was held outside in the football stadium. I would have been outraged if they had moved it inside. I'd rather be wet than cramped. The upside was that they cut out a few of the speeches and went right to the diplomas. When my name was called the crowd cheered "Bear!!!!" (did I ever mention I had a nickname?), I got my diploma (actually just the sleeve, we picked up our diplomas the next day), gave Rev. McMickle (Aaron's father, who's also president of the school board) a big hug, and walked off the stage.

My wrestling career, however, did not end on as high a note. After having a very good dual meet season (went 6–3 in the league) and a year of complete agony, I beat some stiff from

Parma. That win against Parma lifted a huge burden off my shoulders. I think my dad was the only one who knew how much that win meant to me. Unfortunately, I lost in the sectional. It's a double elimination tournament, and I lost both matches by a point. One of my coaches tried to reassure me by telling me how much he enjoyed watching me wrestle, and I almost started to cry. I was extremely disappointed. Despite all that I had gone through in the sport, I always thought I would at least go to districts. I went home that night and had an intimate experience with a bottle of Scotch. I was drunk for the next day and a half. Coach Kornblut really helped me get through those days after my loss, and I'll always appreciate that and everything else he has done for me. I may not have been as close to him, or revered him as much as I did Coach Sedmak, but I owe a lot to Coach Kornblut for sticking with me and always being encouraging.

►

Coach Kornblut
Wrestling Coach

Josh's season turned around when he got into Yale. He had a lot more success. A week and a half later he placed in a very difficult tournament—much more difficult than the one he didn't place in over at Richmond Heights. I was convinced that it was Yale. Yale gave him that extra confidence.

The next few weeks (months to be honest) were very hard for me. I was grouchy, upset, and ashamed. I still am. I really regret not having worked harder at wrestling. I really loved wrestling this year—believe it or not—and I would kill for just one more year of experience. For the first time, I looked forward to going to the room to work out. Hopefully I can take my regrets and turn them into a learning experience. I think that knowing that things really do get better with enough hard work is a valuable lesson that can't be learned too many times.

So school went well, wrestling was both great and terrible, and my social life was somewhere in between. And, get ready: Elena and I hooked up sometime around New Year's! Yes, it finally happened, and we were officially together on January 16. It all started with the Winter Ball. (I know it sounds like a fairy tale, but it's true.) It was a Sadie Hawkins dance, and my friend—and I emphasize the word "friend"—Sarah had asked me. (I found out on Christmas Eve that Elena was planning on asking me, too, but Sarah had beaten her to the punch.) So I went with Sarah and spent the majority of the ball dancing with her, but I couldn't help watching Elena out of the corner of my eye. (Okay, so I was staring.) Eventually we danced together. It was like being in a movie; we talked and joked as we danced. And then it happened. Actually, it could probably use a bit more of an explanation, seeing as it wasn't your normal first kiss. To tell you the mildly embarrassing truth, I had asked her for a piece of gum (my oral fixation always acts up when I'm nervous—I bite my nails till there's nothing left), and she told me to "come and get it." GASP. I know, that's pretty weak—I don't even think anyone on *Saved by the Bell* did that—but that was our first kiss. It was wonderful. It was about time that a girl I was interested in was interested in me.

Things went well for about two months, at which point I began to lose interest. I can't explain it any better than that. Everyone was shocked, including me. Nobody had believed that someone like her would like me in the first place, so you can just imagine how surprised they were when *I* wanted to break up with *her*. I had to avoid Rob in the halls at school, because I just knew he'd call me on it.

I did the deed after spring break, during which I drove from Cleveland to Lansing to Detroit to Cleveland, and flew out to

Florida and back. It was this trip that cinched the decision for me, because during all that travel time I barely thought of Elena except in terms of how to break up with her. I knew that I had to do something, so I broke it off that Monday.

She took the news as well as anyone could. I felt bad and everything, but I would have felt worse if I had strung her along. The funny thing was, before I broke up with her I felt so uncomfortable around her, but the second it was done, it felt exactly like old times, when I was happy just to be around her. I thought it was because we were just friends again. I was positive that we would remain best of friends forever. But I destroyed my little Platonic utopia when I decided that I had been wrong, that I had just been confused, and we should get back together. Of course, I picked the optimum time to tell her all of this, when we were both trashed as hell. I couldn't even finish a sentence because I would forget what I was talking about midway through. She wasn't too happy about me breaking the news this way, and didn't know what to do. Eventually she agreed that we belonged together, and so by May we were going out again. Very eighth grade.

We went to Prom together. I had asked her while we were dating the first time. Even while we were separated we still planned to go together. I had a wonderful time on Prom night, surprisingly enough. And in case you were wondering, our Prom night resembled her dream Prom a lot more than it resembled mine, which was fine by me (honestly). After Prom, though, it was her turn to lose interest. The big problem was that Elena, how should I put this, didn't fulfill all of the requirements of being a couple. I'm not even talking about sex (which hadn't ever been an issue). I'm talking about anything at all. Every time she came over, she would wait for my mom and dad to fall asleep (which I took as a good sign), and then . . . fall asleep. Even on her birthday, when I took her out for a really nice dinner, bought her a teddy bear, and rented *Jerry Maguire*!!!!!! (If I'm going to sit and watch Tom Cruise for two hours, the *least* she could do would be to stay awake.) The first few times it happened, I was a little mad and more than a little frustrated, but not too worried. But when it happened every single time we were together (which was much less often than I would have liked), I started to be concerned. I mean, I am way too young for this kind of problem. After a month (a very, very long month), I decided to bite the bullet and talk to her. I explained all of my feelings to her and basically said that there was no point in our calling ourselves boyfriend and girlfriend if she didn't want to participate in any of the activities that distinguished boyfriends and girlfriends from friends. After several days of protesting that she was still attracted to me but that she was just too tired (yeah, those vacations are murder) or I seemed too tired (me? *never*), and one last nap, she finally came out with it. It was over. I was hurt, and I felt like crap, but I certainly knew where she was coming from. Then, just out of curiosity (and because I *had* to know), I asked her when she had made that decision. A few days ago, she says. A few DAYS ago!?! I was furious. She should have told me instead of letting me believe that things would be okay. Every time I think about it I get red in the face. So that's that. It was nice while it lasted, but it's sure as hell over now.

And then there's Yale, the light of my life. I went out there in April for their Future Freshman Days, which is this program they plan for the applicants who have been accepted. By the time I came home, I was ready to pack right then. The closer I come to going, the more nervous I get. But it's a great kind of nervousness, the kind that keeps you up at night and fills your head with ideas and images of things to come. After all those forms I filled out and nights I spent trying to make myself look good on paper, Yale has ceased to be some abstract land where people are analyzing me and deciding whether I am worthy of its hallowed ground, and has become my future reality. I'm going to live there. With other people. I have roommates—actual people from Connecticut, Virginia, and Costa Rica. I'm very nervous, but even more excited. I leave for a preorientation camping trip in three weeks.

►

Tamara Shirdak
Yale Admissions Officer

When Josh came to our welcoming program, he probably convinced another three or four people to attend Yale, just through sheer enthusiasm. During the scavenger hunt, he worked with some other people who had been accepted through regular admission and therefore didn't have to enroll at Yale and had some other really great options, but since meeting Josh they've enrolled and made plans to start here in the fall. So Josh's obsession really carried through to other people.

I still haven't cleaned my room (I don't even know if it's possible to clean this beast in three weeks), but I guess it won't matter once I'm gone. (Just kidding, Mom.) With that, packing, and the continuing Elena saga, I'll probably be in New Haven before I know it, taking my first step inside the Ivy walls that will frame the next four years of my life. But that's a different story for a different time. I'll write that book when I come to it.

Author's Note (and Reader's Cheat Sheet)

AP—The Advanced Placement program is offered by the College Board. AP courses and tests give high school students the chance to do college-level work in high school and to earn college-level credit by taking and scoring well on AP tests. AP tests are offered in 25 subjects, and are scored from 1 to 5, 3 being passing, 5 being the best score.

Applying early—see Early decision.

College Board—The College Board is a national association that sponsors the SATs, PSATs, and the AP program. I don't really know too much beyond that.

Conference—To recruit students, colleges send representatives of their admissions offices to cities and high schools around the country to hold informational sessions for students interested in learning more about that school. The representatives usually speak for a little while about the school and then take questions.

Early decision—Also called early admission. Some schools give applicants the option of an earlier application deadline (usually around October 15). The catch is that if you get accepted after applying early, you are obligated to attend that school and withdraw all other applications.

ETS (Educational Testing Service)—The organization (I think they're somewhere in New Jersey) that develops and scores standardized tests like the SATs. When you apply anywhere, you have to request that an official score sheet be sent from the ETS to that school.

GPA (grade point average)—This is the method schools use to determine your cumulative average from all of your classes and years of high school. Each letter grade has a numerical equivalent (usually on a scale of 1 to 4, but my high school's went to 4.5). High schools (and colleges, I assume) use these GPAs to choose valedictorians and salutatorians, and admissions committees use them to evaluate applicants.

JV (Junior Varsity)—High school sports have varsity teams, which are generally made up of juniors and seniors, and JV teams, which are freshmen and sophomores. (Of course I was the exception to this rule.)

National Merit—The National Merit Scholarship Corporation gives scholarships based on PSAT scores. (The PSAT is also known as the NMSQT, or National Merit Scholarship Qualifying test.) They have semifinalists and finalists for these scholarships, as well as commending students who did really well but not well enough to qualify. (I was a commended scholar.)

PSAT—The PSAT (Preliminary SAT or NMSQT) is based on the SAT and is structured and scored pretty much the same way. As the College Board will tell you, the PSAT has two main purposes. One, to give the student an idea of what the SAT test will be like without having the scores count toward college admissions, and two, as a way of awarding National Merit Scholarships.

Recommendation—Most college applications require at least two letters of recommendation, where a teacher (or someone else who has known you well as a student) describes and evaluates you, and talks about why you would be good for that school.

Usually people ask their teachers to write the recommendations, but they also can come from coaches or counselors, and some schools even ask for peer recommendations.

SAT (Scholastic Assessment Test)—The infamous three-hour test all colleges require (that or the ACT), and one of the primary ways they choose applicants. It's primarily multiple choice, split up in two sections—math and verbal. Each section is scored out of 800, so a perfect score for the test is 1,600.

SAT II—One-hour, mostly multiple-choice, tests in specific subjects. These tests measure knowledge of particular subjects and the ability to apply that knowledge. Many colleges require or recommend one or more of these tests for admission or placement purposes.

Two-a-days—Intensive football practices that take place at the end of August, right before school starts. They're called two-a-days because the team practices twice a day (really more like all day with a break for lunch, but I guess it just has a nice ring that way).